SNAPSHOTS FROM HEAVEN

Cracking the CAT, MBA and Entrepreneurship Conundrum

SIDDHARTH JAIN

Om Books International

First published in 2026 by

Om Books International

Corporate & Editorial Office
A-12, Sector 64, Noida 201 301
Uttar Pradesh, India
Phone: +91 120 477 4100
Email: editorial@ombooks.com
Website: www.ombooksinternational.com

Sales Office
107, Ansari Road, Darya Ganj,
New Delhi 110 002, India
Phone: +91 11 4000 9000
Email: sales@ombooks.com
Website: www.ombooks.com

ISBN: 978-93-6395-203-4

Printed in India

10 9 8 7 6 5 4 3 2 1

SNAPSHOTS FROM HEAVEN

Siddharth Jain is a dynamic force in technology and entrepreneurship whose journey spans from Goldman Sachs and Morgan Stanley to the innovative realms of start-up leadership. As co-founder and CTO of TruLeague (a Techstars-backed platform transforming higher education enrolment), and Founder at Riverhouse Technologies (an IT Services company specialising in 0 to MVP for start-ups), Siddharth masterfully bridges high-stakes corporate strategy with ground-breaking entrepreneurial ventures.

A proud alumnus of IIM Kozhikode and PESIT Bangalore, Siddharth's diverse experiences have not only sharpened his strategic acumen but have also fuelled his passion for empowering youth. A sought-after mentor, he is dedicated to inspiring future leaders to pursue their dreams with courage and creativity.

Whether he is engaging in a challenging game of poker or energising his day with team sports, Siddharth embodies a balanced approach to life—combining analytical rigour with an enduring creative spirit. His commitment to excellence and genuine desire to uplift others make him a standout figure in both the professional world and beyond.

To my father,
Praduman Jain

Contents

Author's Note

What to and What not to Expect

In a diverse country like India, beyond the everyday conflicts of gender, caste, religion, sexual orientation, and other social attributes, there stands an aspiration that unites all Indians—the aspiration to get into one of the prestigious IITs or IIMs. These institutions are as close as anything to representing "heaven" on earth, both for ambitious students and their doting parents. For this story, let's consider an IIM to be heaven. How does one get into heaven? Through devotion, rites, and rituals. So that's what students end up doing for years.

This book is my effort to build a stairway to heaven for aspiring IIM enthusiasts and to show what it is like. It will help you clarify questions surrounding IIM admissions and present shortcuts/tweaks for CAT and interviews that might help improve your preparation efficiency. It will give you an idea of the ground you need to cover. Believe me, there is no secret ingredient. You just have to have unbound passion and work unceasingly towards it. Not all IIM graduates get in on their first attempt. Some don't get a good enough CAT score, while others get close but lose out in the personal interviews. The ones who make it through attribute it to their sheer dedication and unwillingness to give up.

This book is my IIM story—the innumerable dilemmas in making this decision and insights into life at an IIM. I strongly believe that the invigorating experiences I have had during this journey and how I thrived through them are going to broaden your mindsets and give you a clearer picture of what unfolds in an IIM. The book also recounts some rather unpleasant personal experiences from my time at IIM.

My dearest readers, most of us grow up with the delusion that we need to keep making efforts only until we reach our long-term goals and then relax for the rest of our lives. But think of a stone that is sitting at the top of a mountain peak. No matter how high the stone has managed to reach, only a rolling stone gathers no moss. I was at the top for as long as I could remember and then came a blow—a crisis, both personal and professional, which had the power to break me at the core. I was incredulously toiling to figure out what hit me in the first place. I was caught completely off-guard, amidst a plethora of unfortunate circumstances. Understanding how things unfolded, accepting them, dealing with them, and finally moving on for the better was a journey that brought out the best in me. It taught me how never giving up empowers you to rise to the peak right after a steep fall and gives you the courage to turn an unfavourable event into an opportunity to rise.

When most of my batchmates were gearing themselves up to climb their high-profile corporate ladders, I, at 23, was being thrown punches by life, one after another, even before I could gather myself up. I had started experiencing anxiety attacks. I had never faced anything like it before, even remotely. The mental trauma was worse than any physical pain I had ever experienced. My self-confidence was at an all-time low, and a blanket of worthlessness enveloped me.

The entire batch had left the campus after completing their course, while I was stuck with my degree deferred. After being one of the first few people in the batch to receive a Tier-1 job offer, I was facing uncertainty in my employment with no visibility on the joining date. The humongous education loan repayment had become hazy. The most awaited grad trip with your closest friends (kind of an IIM ritual) seemed like a far-fetched reality distortion.

"How did I end up like this? I didn't even want to do an MBA in the first place. Or was I too gullible in my understanding of heaven? Or maybe I deserve this?" These thoughts echoed in my head as I was lying down on a broken wooden bench beside the isolated lake at the God's Own Campus. Gazing into a starless sky. Unbothered by the darkness around, the anthill near my feet, or the barking of a dog nearby (which could easily have been a fox).

The sudden fall from the top was intractable. Both my personal and professional existence were challenged. It was the perfect test of my character and integrity. And what unfolded was the adventure of a lifetime!

Why MBA?

"I am at a point in my career where I need to holistically develop myself as a human resource. I have gained some exposure in the technical field and feel that it is the perfect time to learn the management side of things. There could be nothing better than a structured formal management education program at a prestigious institute like yours to help me realise my short-term and long-term career goals."

This is a snapshot of most of the "Why MBA?" answers, but to be blunt about it, these answers barely scratch the surface of the truth. These are just structured answers that students rehearse for months with the help of their coaching institutes. The reality is quite different. Quality education is not the only reason that prompts people to pursue an MBA nowadays.

Most people opt for an MBA because they consider the brand value to be imperative for their careers;

it's usually a requirement for that much-coveted job promotion. Most MNCs (Multi-National Companies) need an MBA degree for higher roles along the hierarchy. Others do an MBA because their professional life suddenly becomes stagnant. They are bored with the 9-5 routine and need a break. Going back to college then has a kick to it because it's risky but exciting. In addition to these, some reasons have been as strange as attempting an MBA to escape meddling parents forcing them into arranged marriages. One of my batchmates was one such victim who just couldn't convince his parents that he already was in a relationship. He took matters into his own hands and decided to give MBA a chance.

While there are still others like me, who never wanted to pursue an MBA in the first place. They somehow land up at a B-School because the circumstances played them.

I was in the final year of my Computer Science Engineering at PESIT, Bangalore. I had secured a decent job offer of 13.5 lakhs per annum and my start-up was in its nascent stages. I was reluctant to study further as I felt that the education system in India inevitably puts a leash on you by making you follow a curriculum of courses, most of which hardly add any value to how things should be pursued in real life. It is not thoroughly utilitarian. I already regretted the fact that I was 21 and was still pursuing only the things a guy who has had good grades during high school is supposed to pursue, according to the mainstream Indian mindset. I had become restless to go out into the real world and start making money. I now had to choose between my start-up and the job offer. Simple choice you'd think? I wish.

My father, a successful stockbroker, had other plans. He believed that I had become too complacent with my job offer and was being lured by the fancy world of start-ups. He was not against the idea of starting my own company; he was a first-generation entrepreneur himself, but he felt that I needed to learn more before starting up. And like the stories of prodigal sons, I turned rebellious and decided to chart my own course in life.

Have you seen the Bollywood movie *Badmaash Company*? Some of you might have been too young when the movie got released but it's quite a fun watch. There is a scene picturising Shahid Kapoor and Anupam Kher (Shahid's father). During a heated argument over Shahid's career path, Anupam Kher says, "Do you know what the problem is with you? The problem is not that you are intelligent, it is that you know you are intelligent".

The stubborn Shahid makes a know-it-all face and leaves, creating a permanent rift between the two. The arguments between Papa and I could have easily led to what happened in the movie, but Papa outsmarted me.

A 52-year-old hard-headed businessman, dapper and always vibrant, with an appearance that defied his age but with a wealth of wisdom that was beyond his years. One evening, as I was dithering between the job and my start-up, he called me to his office to glean what was going on in my head. I was prepared to defend myself against his barrage of questions; after all, I just wanted to make my own decisions. I wanted to close the topic of MBA once and for all.

As I entered his office, I had a feeling I was going to lose the conversation for I could see his eagerness for the conversation in the way his head tilted forward and his forearms extended across the walnut veneer of his desk, hands joined together by the interlocking of his fingers. I sat across his desk, slightly laid back on my chair with both my hands resting on my lap, and waited for him to begin. "Siddharth, do you know what the problem is with you? You are intelligent, no doubt, but not as intelligent as you think you are. You are behaving like a fool and you don't even realise it. Do you think that IIMs are not good enough for you? Do you think you are above them? I don't understand what is wrong with you. I'm offering you a deal. You prove to me that you are worthy enough to get selected into these IIMs. Get an admission letter from one of the top IIMs and I promise I shall not force you to join the MBA course. I will leave it up to you."

I was speechless. I was prepared for a fight. But what I got instead was a challenge. There was nothing left for me to argue about. He had presented the most logical argument. It was hard for me to contest his proposal without accepting that maybe I wouldn't be able to get into an IIM. I accepted the challenge. I did put up my counter though. I proposed that if I got him the IIM admission letter, we would take that long pending foreign family vacation that we had been planning for about six years. He agreed and I left his office. My intelligence and my ego had been instrumental in bringing me this far. My father knew this and he used it to his advantage. With our deal in place, I was now determined to get selected for one of the IIMs. I put my start-up on hold for a few months and started working day and night preparing for CAT. I never knew that ego could be such a great motivation to achieve something.

Bell the CAT

CAT preparation tests the best of us. CAT is one of the most competitive exams in the world and preparing for CAT means you inevitably end up preparing for other MBA competitive exams like GMAT as well. Because of this, CAT precedes all others and needs the most focus. Personally, my biggest dilemma in the earlier days was whether I needed to join a coaching centre or prepare on my own.

CAT coaching is helpful but only when you can get the maximum out of a coaching program. This means you need to be very clear about what you want from each session. In a coaching institute, the faculties need to follow a certain structure that is designed to teach the topics in a generalised manner. This in turn means that more often than not, topics will be taught right from their basics to get students from all backgrounds on the same page. It makes less sense for students who already know the basics to attend such classes, that time can be used for practice instead. Such people should probably skip the introductory sessions and attend the sessions where there are advanced questions along with the corresponding shortcuts that can save time while solving them. What is important is that you ask the coaching faculty to give a session schedule/ breakup beforehand so that you know which classes to attend and prepare yourself accordingly to make the most out of those classes. It's about choosing the mode of preparation that is most productive for you. Some aspirants can focus better when part of an organised coaching program, while others learn more effectively on their own. There is no one-size-fits-all strategy. But following someone else blindly will push you one step behind the competition right from the start, avoid that at all costs.

Apart from teaching the CAT curriculum, coaching programs are important because they give you an idea of where you stand as compared to your peers at the national level. The thing that helped me the most in CAT preparation was taking up a series of beautifully designed mock tests that give you an actual feel of the CAT exam. They give you a detailed analysis of your performance and an all-India Percentile gives you a real picture of where you stand amidst your competition. Since you can write these mocks from the comfort of your home, it is a lot more convenient and saves time. It also comes in handy for people who are professionally committed elsewhere and cannot attend coaching classes. The key is to spend at least as much time analysing your performance in the test as you have devoted to writing the actual test. Keep making notes of the shortcuts you discover while studying the solutions for the mock tests and star mark the common mistakes that you have been making. Something as simple as the fact that 8% of 25 is the same as 25% of 8 is a shortcut that often does not come to mind while solving questions under stress. Writing it down as a note increases your chances of being able to use it when it matters. These notes should be the bible that you need to revisit before every mock test and the final CAT as well. The stronger your notes, the more confident you will be before any exam.

I scored a 98 percentile in my first mock with minimal preparation but that did not remain a constant. When you start, you realise that you are strong in some topics while weak in others. There is always an element of luck involved. The scores went down to as low as 71 on unlucky days when the mock test contained more questions from my weaker topics and kept fluctuating. With every mock test, a pattern of your strengths and weaknesses begins to appear. Focusing on individual sections and sub-sections depending on these patterns is quite a low-hanging fruit to improve your CAT score. You need to keep working on your weaker topics until even your luck becomes insignificant. Also, you mustn't become complacent with the high scores or lose hope with the low scores. Once you have decided to do an

MBA, do what it takes to bell the CAT. CAT is not like IIT-JEE where the technical syllabus itself seems infinite. CAT is more about speed and accuracy. If your basics till the 10th standard are strong, you already have an edge over the competition. You have to streamline your preparation. Don't just read and solve whatever comes your way, build a structure that translates into higher mock scores for you and devote your time accordingly. Half your battle is won if you can successfully correlate your strengths and weaknesses with your performance and then use the same to score better in the next mock. This combined with serious practice is the Kingmaker for anybody who wants to excel in CAT.

There are three sections in CAT:

1. Quantitative Ability (QA) which deals with mathematics (this is your basic 10th standard maths) and general aptitude.
2. Data Interpretation and Logical Reasoning (DI/LR) where DI deals with the interpretation of data in graphs and other charts while LR looks at logical puzzle solving.
3. Verbal Ability and Reading Comprehension (VA/RC) where VA is about testing your English language skills while RC deals with understanding paragraphs on a topic/story and making the most logical inferences out of it.

Proceed with the preparation section-wise. For Quantitative Ability, be done with reading the course material at the very beginning of your preparation, so that there is nothing you don't know about. In my personal opinion, the rest of the Quantitative Ability and the other two (VA/RC and DI/LR) sections can be scaled solely by practice. Also learning by practising/giving tests is more efficient in terms of making good use of the time you can devote to CAT preparation. Specifically for the VA/RC section, read as much as you can and start as early as you can. If people in high school are reading this, don't think that you will prepare for CAT after/during your undergraduate studies. The more you read the better. Read whatever interests you but also read the editorial pages of reputed national dailies. Paragraphs will naturally start making sense to you once you are into the habit of reading, and the comprehension time improves drastically. Start now. It is a myth that questions in VA/RC are open to interpretation and hence, tough to answer correctly. Once you have read a decent amount of intellectually stimulating material, every question in VA/RC can be answered objectively. Be it the logical sequences, para-jumble, or summary questions, an objective approach will push you to improve your accuracy by eliminating any ambiguities in decision-making. The more you practise and analyse the solutions, the more your mind will start thinking in terms of eliminating options and choosing the best answer. This practice grows into your subconscious and comes out as a gut feeling on D-Day, which essentially is an objective approach that you developed over time.

The final advice to bell the CAT is strategising. You can't just practice without a strategy and hope to get lucky while writing the CAT exam. Often, you will find yourself stuck in a situation where you can eliminate 2 options out of 4 but are still left with 2 other options, which you think could be correct with equal probability. What do you do then? Do you take the chance (of course risking the negative marking) or do you play safe and leave it un-attempted? How do you make a logical decision in such a scenario? A logical decision can be taken after understanding the following facts.

First of all, you need to know how much score you need. Let's say, you are aiming for a 99 percentile in CAT. Based on previous years' patterns, you can find the target score for yourself. Taking my case as an example, it was 180/300. Now, CAT's marking scheme is +3, -1, for a total of 100 questions. So, for a 180 score, a rough calculation suggests attempting 80% of the questions with 80% accuracy. Explanation: you attempt 80 questions out of 100. For 80% accuracy, 64 will be correct and 16 will be wrong. With a +3, -1 marking scheme, your score is 64*(+3) + 16*(-1) = 176, roughly close to the 99-percentile mark. If you have this calculation in mind, i.e., the number of attempts and the accuracy %, you can make a calculated decision about taking risks in the exam. Based on the mock tests, you can also analyse whether you need to work on improving your number of attempts or the accuracy.

One strategy that I followed to make use of the above fact is this: attempt the CAT exam in three rounds. In round one, only attempt the questions which you think can be easily solved and for which you are confident about the accuracy. Also, keep marking the questions which you think can be solved but will take some time, to review later. In round two, attempt all the questions marked for review in round one. Now, only answer the questions you are sure about in round two, and leave others marked for review. Here is where the risk calculation will also come into the picture. After the two rounds, estimate a rough score for yourself. Then begin round three. If you are around your target, 180 in this case, don't take any more risks. If you are falling a little short, take a few risks that can help you cross your target. If you are way below the target, you should take more risks. As an example, a score of +99 or -100 will be the same for you (this can be different for different people), but I hope you get my point. If you are below the score you need or the cut-off score, doesn't matter how far below you are, better to take more risks and hope to get lucky while marking the options.

The three-round strategy worked for me and works for many others, but don't use it if it doesn't work for you. What I am advising is that plan and decide whatever strategy works for you, but do have a strategy. Use the mock tests to try out different strategies for yourself and finally choose to go with the one that gives you maximum results. Don't go for a CAT or any other entrance exam without a strategy. That will take away any edge that you might have in the first place.

Also, let me shed some light on how negative marking works. Have you ever wondered how the +3, -1 marking scheme came into play? What is its significance? Let's say a person doesn't know how to answer any question in CAT but is over-smart at the same time. He decides to mark answers for all 100 questions as option C, thinking that probability-wise, at least 25 questions will be correct. Let's calculate a score for such a person. For all answers marked C, assuming equal distribution for all options being correct, he will get 1/4th, i.e., 25 questions correct and 75 questions wrong. Score = 25*(+3) + 75(-1) = 0. A fair score for such a person. The +3, -1 marking scheme doesn't incentivise or de-incentivise you to take any risks. Probability-wise, it doesn't add to your score or take away from it. Had the marking scheme been +4/-1, an aspirant would have had more incentives to take risks. Likewise, had the marking scheme been +3/-2, the aspirant would have had negative incentives to take risks. All these facts running inside your subconscious mind, strongly help you strategize for CAT. By practising even the smallest sectional tests using these guidelines, your brain becomes accustomed to attempting CAT in a manner that will give you optimum results in the final CAT exam.

CAT does not test what you have learned in the last year of preparation, it tests what you have learned right from the time you started learning, which resonates directly with the expected traits of an MBA. On a philosophical note, a strong leader becomes strong not because of the experiences of a year or two, but because of learnings throughout his life.

I started preparing sincerely in August 2015 and in the little time I had left till November, I tried to take as many mock tests as I could. CAT mostly coincides with semester-end exams during under-graduation. For me, CAT was on 29th November 2015 and the final exams started on 1st December 2015. Along with that, the subject I dreaded the most "Web Technologies" was the first exam. I am sincerely grateful to my friends who helped me study one day before to get a 9-pointer in that exam. They helped me design a readymade code structure that could be built upon to answer most of the coding questions. They even shortlisted important theory topics for me. I have always been blessed when it comes to forming true friendships through the different phases of my life. Having said that, it's highly recommended that you plan and prepare well in advance to balance the two, the CAT and your final exams.

Right after CAT, I resumed my work on the start-up. That is what I had wanted to do in the first place. I had gone all-in for CAT but like a game of poker, the results were not in my hand. Even if I did score a good percentile, admission into an IIM would still only have been to prove my capability to my father. But probably because of the effort I had made towards CAT, the thought of an IIM MBA soon started niggling into my daily thoughts. It made the dilemma of choosing between a start-up and an MBA only worse with time.

I don't know if it was a coincidence or a play of destiny, but the CAT results came exactly at the time when I was finalising a website development deal for my start-up, over a phone call. I scored a 99.02 percentile. I didn't know whether to be happy or sad about it. I called Papa and informed him. Something that I had never expected to happen, happened. In his elated voice, he said, "Siddharth, I am proud of you. You have done tremendously well and have proved yourself. Although nobody would be happier than me if you go for an MBA, I will not force you anymore. It's up to you whether you want to prepare for the interviews or not. I am with you in whatever you wish to pursue." Even before the interview round, my father held up his end of the bargain and we went on a family vacation to Thailand. Scuba diving, underwater walking, parasailing, white water rafting, and snorkelling in the beautiful islands of Thailand, surely was the experience of a lifetime.

But once I was back, I was suddenly in the throes of the biggest dilemma of my professional life. I had to take this decision on my own, and ironically, it was a daunting task. The independence to make my own decision was strangely exhilarating and scary. Hadn't this been what I had wanted in the first place? I had no time; I had to make a choice soon. While working for the start-up, I realised that I lacked expertise in multiple areas and needed formal training in those. Without some specific skill sets, you often find yourself looking for help from the outside. You become dependent. Apart from that, irrespective of the fact that some dropouts and people with ordinary education have done well in their lives, the percentage is very small. The market still looks for credibility and a Management degree from a prestigious institute always helps.

My fear of missing out was tremendous. I was afraid to let go of my 99-percentile score in CAT and that fear in turn motivated me to start preparing for the IIM interviews. All this while I kept working on my start-up.

The interview round involves an assessment of your entire profile built through your formative years. This leads to many questions in the minds of every IIM aspirant. I would like to dedicate the next two chapters to answering the two most common questions people have during their preparations.

- On the importance of grades
- On choosing between pursuing an MBA before or after work experience

So many people give their opinions that students have a hard time making collective sense of them. These chapters should help IIM aspirants and their parents make well-informed decisions.

Grades Don't Matter?

One of the biggest questions we have during our schooling years is, "Do grades matter?" This is a question that troubles both extremes of people, students with low grades who feel insecure about their prospects and the ones with top grades who constantly question whether their effort to score higher grades is worth it. The problem in dealing with these questions is that our minds have been trained to find generalised answers to questions that cannot be generalised. Let me give you an honest perspective on this without mincing words so that you are more informed while making your choices. Oftentimes we casually hear people say that grades don't matter. What they mean is that grades should not matter, and we happily assume that grades have no value in the real world.

A lot of students aren't aware that IIMs give weightage to 10th grades, 12th grades, and under-graduation grades during admission. The weightage is good enough to make or break your admission into your dream Institute. But should grades be given weightage for admission into courses like MBA? Can't a person who did not score well in 10th and 12th be a deserving candidate for an MBA from one of the top Institutes in India? Or does a student with average or low grades not deserve a well-paying job? I agree that grades don't define a person and low grades do not imply that the person does not deserve to be successful. But there is a reason for giving weightage to grades. When recruiters come to campus, they don't have the time and the resources to scan each one of the profiles. Time wasted is money wasted for them. So, it's not that the recruiters consider low CGPA students as unworthy of the job, it's just cost-efficient for them to shortlist people based on grades. Likewise, MBA institutes need to have some filter to ease the process of selection. Grades are seen as a means of indicating consistency in your schooling years. Whether you like it or not, the harsh reality is that grades do matter, at least for mainstream courses like MBA. I am not saying that a person with low grades can't succeed on a mainstream career path, but it's tougher in the beginning. That person has to knock on a lot more doors initially. Once he is in his field, then only his work matters.

For non-mainstream (broadly referring to courses other than Engineering, Commerce, Medical, and Management) courses, the grades should not and do not matter to a large extent. It is only fair because people who are ambitious about their non-mainstream careers often spend a lot of time perfecting their skills/passion which takes a toll on their mainstream grades. But it is naïve to think that because the grades don't matter, it is easy to succeed in a non-mainstream career. In reality, it's comparatively easier to succeed in a mainstream career. Because here, your paths are defined, while, in non-mainstream careers, you often have to create paths for yourself. You need that extra motivation to keep working towards your goals even when you aren't sure about the results. Just take the example of book publishing. It's quite straining to be able to write a book, land a publisher, and eventually make money out of it for a living. You face rejection more than a mainstream student can imagine and I can say this because I have been a part of both sides now. I have been at the top of my mainstream career but faced infinite struggles to get this book published. 100 words, 500 words, 1000 words, you keep setting short-term targets and writing your story, then suddenly it doesn't make sense and you have to delete it all. Even when you manage to stay motivated and complete writing a book, you realise that the battle is not even half won. You have to go through editors, literary agents, and publishers and if you are lucky, you get your work published. It's a strenuous experience, at least for a first-time author like me. It is normal for the process to take at least a year and this is after you have completed writing the first draft of the book. Rejection becomes a habit but success comes eventually only when the passion is kept alive. Irrespective of external circumstances, you have to believe in what you want to do and that can only happen when you are true to yourself and true to the purpose of pursuing your goals. If anybody wants to become a writer or choose a non-mainstream path just because you can't get good grades, you are way off the mark, and it is next to impossible for you to succeed. Letting go of good grades is justified only when it happens organically and when you are making better use of the time you would have spent scoring those grades.

Having said that, as far as getting admission into an IIM is concerned, the most important thing is to have a single-minded focus to follow your ambitions. It is even more important than having good grades. The do-what-it-takes attitude is inevitable if you dream of entering into an IIM or any other prestigious institute, for that matter. The competition is fierce. There will always be people working harder, longer, and smarter than you. The day you start taking things for granted even a little, is the day you should forget about achieving your dream. Believe in karma and don't look back once you have decided to tread the difficult path. I can assure you, it will all be worth it!

The Fresher vs Work Experience Debate

MBA before work or work before MBA? While contemplating pursuing an MBA from one of the IIMs, a lot of us face a big dilemma: to go for an MBA right after graduation, or work for a few years and then do an MBA. After spending two eventful years with a batch of highly diverse people in terms of work experience, I learned the pros and cons of each.

For those of you who are unaware of the MBA jargon, a fresher at an IIM is a person who joins the Institute right after under-graduation, without any work experience. In monetary terms, a fresher has an edge. Let's take the scenario of a 22-year-old who has 2 options: work for 2 years (average work experience in the batch) and then join an MBA course or join an MBA directly after undergraduation. I'll present a

5-year comparative scenario and the financial impact of joining an IIM as a fresher versus with work experience.

- Scenario 1 (With Work Experience): The average annual package that people leave to join an IIM is around ₹5-6 lakhs.The individual earns ₹10-12 lakhs over 2 years before spending ₹25 lakhs on an MBA. After graduation, they secure a ₹20 lakh package (decent IIM package assumption), resulting in a net gain of ₹7 lakhs (+12-25+20) over 5 years. I have not taken living expenses into account because they will be the same in both scenarios.
- Scenario 2 (As a Fresher): The individual directly invests ₹25 lakhs in an MBA, then earns ₹20 lakhs annually (a fair assumption because package opportunities are equal for freshers and people with work experience) for 3 years, leading to a net gain of ₹35 lakhs (-25+20+20+20), even ignoring yearly salary appraisals.

This pure mathematical interpretation shows that by the age of 27 (5 years from the start), the person who joined as a fresher would have made ₹28 lakhs (35-7) more than the person who joined after work experience. While this difference isn't massive over 5 years, it highlights key financial considerations based on short- and long-term priorities. I know it sounds too money-minded, but who are we kidding? We are talking about an MBA and you just can't ignore the monetary aspect while considering an MBA. At the end of these

5 years, it is an equal playing field for the people in both scenarios after which only individual performance determines future growth.

In terms of academics, it's a little easier for a fresher to adjust to the B-School vigour as they are still in the habit of studying regularly for long hours. At the same time, it's easier for a person with work experience to grasp concepts in class because of previous exposure, resulting in better class participation and project performance. The pedagogy followed by most B-Schools employs case studies to teach management concepts and people with work experience should relate it to the real world. On one hand, freshers tend to be unbiased and have a raw mindset while approaching new ideas, while on the other hand, people with work experience are more realistic in their approach and put forward more practical solutions. This also helps people with experience to win case competitions that happen across different B-Schools and are mostly organised by different companies recruiting on campus.

In terms of people relationships, people with work experience have an edge because after being exposed to the corporate world, they understand the more important things in life. Freshers are more competitive and more focused on grades, in general. At a B-School where networking predominantly relates to your bread and butter in the future, people with work experience are more skilled in building fruitful relationships while on campus. They know how to establish a balance between competition amongst peers, studies, and people relationships.

Also, because of more financial independence, people with work experience often end up enjoying life at the campus a little more. Freshers are still dependent on their families not so much for getting money (because bank loans provide for personal expenses as well) but for money management in general. So, they are always accountable for how they are spending their money. This is not a point substantial enough to influence your decision of when to do an MBA but is still presented to give you an idea of the basic nuances of B-School life.

When it comes to placements, freshers have a lot more choices. If you have prior work experience, the placements' committee will pitch you to recruiters in similar domains of your work experience and your profiles will be locked accordingly. Opting for a different domain than the one during your work experience is a risk that people are highly discouraged from taking because of brutal competition. Freshers have an open feast of choices during placements and they can explore sitting for companies from totally different sectors. A lot of finance and marketing roles prefer freshers. I made a keen observation during the placements; when a marketing company chooses a fresher over a guy who has experience in marketing before an MBA, the experienced guy more often than not starts taking offense, "How could the company disregard my relevant experience and choose a fresher over me? Do these freshers even know anything?" I am sharing these dialogues as first-hand experiences and not hearsay. I didn't know the answer to this during my MBA, however, today I can answer this because I have been on the other side of the table now and have recruited multiple times for my own companies. Let's carry the marketing role assumption forward and let's further narrow it down to a digital marketing role at an FMCG company. Now, as a recruiter, let's say I have two choices. First, a person who has worked in a digital marketing company for 2 years before the MBA, and second, a person who has no work experience before the MBA at all, i.e., a fresher. My major point of analysis would be: How much time will this fresher take to learn what the experienced guy has learned in two years? If the fresher's analytical and intellectual skills can convince me that he could learn most of those digital marketing concepts in 6 months, I would prefer recruiting that fresher even when he knows less at this point. Logically, yes, I would need to invest 6 months in the fresher but after 6 months, the guy who is a faster learner would yield exponential results for the company. The initial 6 months would be more than compensated for. I am not trying to say that freshers are more intelligent in any way; that would be a foolish and naïve assumption. The point I am trying to make here is that having work experience is not a trump card which could give you an easier entrance into your choice of companies. It is an equal playing field and more about "survival of the fittest" than anything else.

I have presented most of the important facts relevant to this debate and you can choose which side you want to be on, nothing right or wrong about it. Nonetheless, I would go ahead and present my personal choice and advice for anybody who wants to join a B-School and is struggling for an answer.

I strongly suggest joining a B-School as a fresher if you can beat the competition. Yes, work experience would help you to understand one or two courses better, but the other courses would still be new for you. Plus, a traditional IT company work experience where you are working just to gain the stamp of work experience will not help you in learning any course better in any way. A guy with experience in finance will still have to learn all the new marketing courses and vice-versa. Work experience only makes sense when you passionately want to work in the role you are working, no point in working just for a stamp.

Moreover, MBA education is costly in India and the fee keeps increasing year after year. So, the earlier you do your MBA, the less pressure on you to get a stable job and clear your loans. In simple terms, it's easier for a person to deal with a loan of 25 lakhs at 23-24 years of age than for someone who is say, 28. At a younger age, you can afford to take more risks even after taking a loan. You find yourself under less pressure in case you don't land yourself a plush job as per your expectations. In the Indian context, getting a stable job and settling down matters a lot to most of us.

I have compiled a list of three reasons, that according to me, justify delaying your MBA after undergraduation:

- You are not sure that you want to pursue an MBA
- You couldn't get into an Institute of your choice
- You have financial constraints

You might ask then, why is it that freshers only constitute 20-25% of the batch size? That's because, as a fresher, you need to have a really strong profile to get admitted into an IIM. There are points for work experience and freshers score a 0 there. Unless you have some extraordinary achievements, it is really hard to beat the competition as a fresher. Most of the people with work experience start writing CATs during their graduation. It's just that it takes multiple attempts to get into an institute of their choice because of the very low acceptance rate. It's a naïve assumption that since the majority of people at an IIM have work experience, people should work before and then join an IIM. Please get your reasoning right, irrespective of whatever decision you choose to make.

By no means do I intend to convey that everybody should just rush toward an MBA right after graduation. Take your time to weigh your options and the dreams you want to pursue. But once you are sure of pursuing an MBA, the sooner you do it, the better. I was plain lucky and blessed to land at the right place at the right time because of my father but a lot of us are bound to make mistakes while making this decision. Hence, it is of utmost importance that after completing my course, I share my honest realisations with my readers, especially all IIM enthusiasts and their parents. After all, these are the experiences that motivated me to write this book in the first place.

Parents, teachers, coaching institutes, relatives (or that annoying and nosy aunty who is sadly your neighbour), so many people advise you during the biggest dilemma of your life. But you need to be smart enough to question the logic behind every statement they make. A lot of people give you advice just because they have heard it from someone else and are mindlessly passing it on to you. A lot of them just want you to believe in what the herd believes. Whatever you choose to do, make sure you do justice with the time and efforts you are devoting towards it.

D-Day

I made sure that I went to every interview with a relaxed mind. The interviews happened in posh settings at 5-star hotels, where you are all suited up and suddenly start feeling like a part of the elite club. However, I did not let the hype of an IIM interview and the fear of failure overcome me. I treated the interview days like normal days. One myth about IIM interviews is that since an MBA is related to management, your undergraduate knowledge will not be tested. This is far from true. The interviewers ask all kinds of technical questions about all the subjects you have dealt with during your undergraduation. This is to test how diligently you have been pursuing the courses that you chose for yourself. You have to be thorough with all your subjects. Special care needs to be taken when the interviewer asks about your favourite subject as most follow-up questions will be based on that. So, it is important to choose your answers wisely.

To satisfy your inquisitiveness, I will share what I answered for the most cliched question asked during the IIM interview: Why an MBA?

- To scale up my start-up which was in its nascent stages
- To expand my father's financial services business
- I wanted to become a writer in the future and an IIM degree would give me the brand value I needed

Although the MBA would have helped me get closer to these aspirations, they were not my driving forces to start preparing for the IIMs. My biggest driving force was my ego; had it not been for my father's wit and my ego, I would never have cleared CAT in the first place.

There are puzzle questions in the interview as well. I was asked the following puzzle in one of my IIM interviews: "You are in a dark room. There are 50 coins placed on a table, out of which 10 coins show tails and 40 coins show heads. Divide this set into two groups (not necessarily of the same size) such that both groups have the same number of coins showing tails." Fortunately, I had dealt with similar logical puzzles during my Engineering placements for software development roles and was able to answer this one correctly.

If an interviewer asks you about a puzzle you have already heard before, never confess that you might know it from before. Act like you are hearing it for the first time and even when you already know the answer, keep talking about it and keep thinking. Finally giving an answer that is very close to the correct answer, is a very tricky task. It is not easy to pull this off in front of the smart IIM professors, but the bonus points it will fetch you, are worth the risk. Better than getting an unknown puzzle thrown at you that you are unable to solve, which will eventually end up lowering your confidence for other parts of the interview also.

All the extra clubs you joined in school/college, all the competitions you won, all the sports you excelled at, and all the internships you did, will now come into play and drive your interview. The interview round has points for extra-curricular activities that you have pursued in the past and the interviewers will be keen on understanding what you learned from those experiences. It is important to understand that the quality of your certificates and not the quantity, is what makes a difference. I had pursued a month-long internship at SAIL (Steel Authority of India Limited) after my 2nd year of Engineering but had hardly gained anything out of the experience other than the certificate. I removed the certificate before going for IIM interviews because I didn't want one certificate to ruin things for me. They would have asked me questions related to the internship and I would not have had any answers. Zero contribution of a certificate is still better than a negative contribution. If you have a certificate that you have gotten without any learning/hard work, it is not going to be of any use to you, and believe me, it's harder to fool the interviewer than you think. For IIM enthusiasts who still have time, start engaging yourselves in extra-curricular activities and try to excel in them. Try and hold positions of responsibility, they have the most points and will even help you during placements once you join an IIM. Again, a position of responsibility just for the sake of it wouldn't help you. If you say you headed some team while organising a college fest, it should be backed by numbers. The number of people who attended the event, the number of sponsors and how you got them, how you managed the budget, the challenges, and the learnings, you need to have experienced those things to answer such questions. If you are good at debating, make sure you represent your school at the bare minimum and earn a certificate from a reputed organisation. If you are into sports, choose a sport and try to play at the national/state level. Only then, it is going to help you in the interviews. Being a jack of all is fine, but a master of at least one is always an added advantage, and in a lot of cases, the difference maker. A lot of students will have top grades and be graduating from top undergraduate colleges, you need to have some unique and extraordinary pointers in your profile to beat the competition.

Also, if you are a GEM (General Engineer Male) like me, buckle up and prepare to work harder than everybody else because you will have no preference whatsoever. It's easier to make excuses that you couldn't make it because of being a GEM but the excuses can help while dealing with others, not yourself.

There was added pressure on me because, in the eyes of family and friends, communication was my strength and all of them had assumed that CAT was the only hurdle I needed to cross to get into an IIM. They felt it would be relatively easy for me to crack the interviews. I kept my calm and was determined to give my best in every interview to avoid any regrets later.

Choosing an IIM is not a big task as they have a standard relative ranking amongst them. You choose the best-ranked IIM according to your calls in most cases unless someone has a specific locational or other personal preference. I had a 9-9-9 profile, meaning 90% or above in 10th, 12th, and under-graduation (the maximum you can have), a 99+ percentile in CAT, my start-up, extra-curricular achievements throughout school and college, and had held multiple positions of responsibility. Still, because of being a GEM and a Fresher (remember the 0 points for work experience?), my IIM (ranked among the top five IIMs then) was the best interview call I had gotten after CAT.

The IIM organised a Group Discussion Round and then an interview round, where the interviewers asked questions related to every line mentioned in my profile and beyond. It was intense and a lot of fun at the same time. The interview concluded with a smile on both the interviewers' faces, which sure wasn't an easy feat to achieve.

I had always believed communication to be my strength and failing at something you believe to be your strength is one of the most demoralising things to happen to you. This highly elevated my eagerness for the results. However, holding onto my confidence during the challenging conversations in the interview and keeping faith in my preparations eventually paid off. I got the much-needed admission letter from one of the top 5 IIMs and now I had to choose whether to go for an MBA or not.

After a few days of indecision, I went to Papa, who was reading in his bedroom after a stressful day at work, and explained to him how hard and stressful it was becoming for me to decide whether to accept or reject that admission letter. He understood that I needed his counsel and I remember his words vividly: "Your coming to me for advice means that somewhere deep down, you are convinced that you should not leave an opportunity to pursue a course which majority of the Indian youth can only dream of. You just want me to say it. You just want me to reassure you that what you are thinking is right. I will go ahead and do exactly that. Pursuing a course from one of the most reputed B-schools in the country will not stop you from following any of your passions. It will only make you more capable of working towards them. You are too young to settle down into a full-time business, you should not have any regrets later. Moreover, the exposure gained from the diversity at IIM will make you a more mature professional and build credibility. Son, you have achieved the IIM dream and you deserve to live it. Don't let go of it."

I decided to move forward with my gut along with Papa's advice and join the Indian Institute of Management. As I was walking out of his bedroom, I had a sudden realisation. I paused for a second, turned around, looked at him, and said, "Right from the time when you hurt my ego to the time when you asked me to decide myself, you knew how this episode would eventually turn out, right? All this while, you had just been tactfully playing me into making the right decision?" He had a mischievous grin on his face when he said, "Tera Baap hu Beta (I am your father, son). Love you."

I convinced him to let me take an educational loan for my MBA. I wanted to take the monetary responsibility of the course myself. I strongly felt that the motivation to repay my educational loan would help bring out the best in me, in terms of what I could achieve at the IIM. Today, after having completed this journey, I can't thank Papa enough for making me live that dream. A dream, that I had not even seen in the first place. The IIM journey was full of ups and downs, which in turn, taught me how to handle success and deal with failure at the same time. It gave me the strength to deal with the harshest of circumstances and turn every setback into an opportunity. More than anything else, it taught me the power of "Karma". I couldn't have imagined spending my most formative years in a more productive and enriching manner.

Some of you still scratching your heads with the interview puzzle? Let me refresh your memory:

"You are in a dark room. There are 50 coins placed on a table, out of which 10 coins show tails and 40 coins heads. Divide this set into two groups (not necessarily of the same size) such that both groups have the same number of coins showing tails."

A: "Randomly divide the coins into two groups of 40 coins and 10 coins each. Now, flip all the coins in the group with 10 coins."

Wondering why this is the answer? If the 10 coins were initially all showing tails, after flipping, there would be 0 coins showing tails in this group as well as 0 coins showing tails in the other group. If there were 9 coins showing tails in the group with 10 coins, after flipping, there would only be 1 coin showing tails in this group and the other group already has 1 coin showing tails. Would urge all of you to hunt for 50 coins and play around with this solution.

The IIM Experience

On the 25th of June 2016, as I entered the gates of the Indian Institute of Management, there was a sense of gratification. It's a feeling that cannot be expressed in words. The campus is a beauty, no less than a luxury resort. It's built up on top of two hills, enveloped by lush green flora. I was prepared to have the best two years of my student journey.

I reached the hostel area and immediately started looking for the warden's office to get my room allocation done. To my surprise, the guard informed me that there was no warden, no office, and we were on our own. Co-ed hostels were run by the students with absolutely zero faculty involvement. This was a drastic shift from Engineering hostels with restrictions, in-timings, and "disciplinary" precautions. The movie *2 States* started making much more sense after all. I later found out that these B-Schools believe in self-regulation by students as being better than any other form of regulation. At a higher level, of course, there is faculty involvement to deal with students' affairs and enforce disciplinary policies, but at the ground level, B-School students are expected to be mature enough to be able to take care of themselves. It doesn't make sense to keep hand-holding the students if the expectation from B-Schools is churning out professionals who are ready for the real world.

The journey kickstarted with *Roobaroo*, a week-long management and cultural fest, where sections compete with each other for glory while showcasing their talents and creativity. The aura is filled with unbridled energy and raw enthusiasm. The way we shed our inhibitions and gelled up to work as teams were the best icebreakers to acclimatise ourselves into the new atmosphere. There were events ranging from dance competitions to extempore debating, from pitching start-up plans to a sale fest where you could sell anything and everything.

Then there was sledging; it involved public humiliation of the performers to discourage them from giving their best. People pulled all-nighters to create witty and vulgar slogans specifically targeted towards individual teams, not just to demotivate the competitors but also to cheer their own. These slogans were then printed on sheets of paper and distributed across the audience to be recited with utmost vigour and passion. The sledging was without any filters and thus not for the weak-hearted. Heated arguments all around, cutthroat competition, banging of drums, and blowing of trumpets added to the overall enthusiasm. The section war only got more intense and fiercer with every other event. *Roobaroo* was by far the most eclectic experience I have ever had.

The last time I had sung on stage was in 5th standard and there I was, singing *Rock On* in the midst of one of the most elite audiences in the country. I had never done a ramp walk in my life and suddenly, I was *The Godfather*, opening the Fashion Parade. Each event was an experience in itself. Winning the competition was a matter of utmost respect and pride for the participants and their section mates.

While the hangover of *Roobaroo* was still alive in the air, reality knocked at our doors in the form of academics. The MBA course is divided into 6 terms distributed over 2 years. Term I was arguably the most tedious and exhaustive term of all. For engineers like me, the courses were mostly all new. Apart from these terms, there is a mandatory summer internship of 2 months between Term III and Term IV. The placements for these internships happened right after Term I. So, preparations for them had to go hand in hand with managing Term I academics. I still didn't know if I wanted to run for placements. So, I shortlisted only a handful of firms that had always been dream companies for me and decided to work hard only for them. The Investment banking role at Silverlight (name changed) was one of the most sought-after and demanding roles on campus. It soon became the next "heaven" I wanted to reach.

Another reason for working hard for placements was the fact that I wanted to know my true capabilities. I wanted to prove to myself, that I was capable of fighting the toughest and still achieving what I wanted. Before the actual courses started, there was a small orientation period that introduced us to the basics of a few courses. While the Quantitative Analysis course was a cakewalk and a major confidence booster for engineers (who are usually in the majority at an IIM) like me, it was a nightmare for those with non-mathematical backgrounds. The quant basics were needed for a lot of other courses in the two-year MBA.

Then there was a case study class by Prof. Unnithan who is one of the most revered marketing professors on campus. Teaching via case studies was a new pedagogy for most of us. Every case study presented a corporate problem and the interactions/viewpoints of the decision-makers while getting to the most optimum solution. They usually didn't involve right or wrong answers but were about understanding the student's opinions about the decisions made in those case studies. It inspired new thought processes among us. Prof. Unnithan taught us a basic workflow to which we needed to devote ourselves, to make the most out of a case study. Right from pre-reading to utilising the class session to clear doubts, present our opinions, and understand others' viewpoints, to post-reading and analysis, he taught us everything. The best part throughout the MBA was that we never dealt with fictional case studies. The case studies always consisted of real corporate examples and gave us insights into how things unfolded in the real world. We were put in the shoes of the top CEOs and asked to make crucial company decisions. At times, we often engaged in role plays where we would take up positions of different characters (a CEO, an advertisement agency, the creative head, a supply manager, a customer relationship manager, an employee, a customer, and so on) in the case study and then have group/class discussions. Deciding what was best for the company with so many stakeholders involved was a task, both challenging and thrilling at the same time. It taught us the practical managerial skills needed to run and grow a real company. On top of that, most of them were the same case studies that were taught at Harvard Business School.

The most life-changing course at the IIM was "Social Transformation in India (STI)", by Prof. Mathew. Prof Mathew is one of the most renowned and loved professors in India and is frequently invited for guest lectures by universities across the globe. He was recently invited to deliver the annual lecture at Brown University (Ivy League), USA. Even before I attended his first lecture, I had seen my seniors wearing t-shirts with Mathew Sir's picture, bearing the quote "Life before and after Mathew". All of us were very keen to meet this person and attend his lecture. Finally, D-Day arrived, I entered the classroom and I am not even exaggerating, I had never seen a classroom like that before! The classroom had turned into an auditorium, with no place to even step foot. Seniors and students from other sections were sitting on the steps, all of them eagerly waiting for the one and only, Prof. Mathew. Luckily, at the IIM, we have designated seats for every student in the first year. I quickly reached my seat and sat there comfortably. The astounding energy in the room only contributed to my increased curiosity to see what the fuss was all about.

A 6'4" tall, slightly dark, well-built man with sharp eyes and a cheerful smile on his face, blushing a little because of the frenzied crowd waiting for him, entered the classroom in his iconic solid black t-shirt and a dark blue pair of jeans. Students went berserk. At my IIM, there is a culture of banging the desks as a symbol of appreciation instead of clapping. As Prof Mathew entered the room, all of us were banging the desks, non-stop; he was welcomed like a celebrity. Honestly, I don't remember hearing a louder banging of desks throughout my PGDM course. It was electrifying. He confidently walked towards the podium, sipped his coffee, and began. There was already something very calming about his presence. He started speaking and we were glued to our seats for the next 75 minutes. Our eyes were gazing at him and our minds were blown away. For the first time in my life, I realised the value of education which is capable of making human beings better for the real world.

He focused on topics which are considered taboos in society. He would intermittently make some very offensive statements and then leave us speechless by saying, "Don't be mad at me. These are not my words. I am just quoting what's written in the holy book 'x' on page number 'y' in line 'z'." He once randomly started picking guys and asked the difference between sanitary pads and tampons. Initially, it made us uncomfortable but as the course progressed, we felt like fools for having resisted ourselves from understanding what is only natural and talking about issues of utmost relevance.

Sir once requested any one of the guys to volunteer to be eve-teased by him. Before he began, he asked all the guys to imagine themselves in the volunteer's place. The volunteer's height, skin colour, hands, legs, hips (read ass), neck, eyes, walk, and even his sexual appeal were objectified without any sophistication filters by Sir; poor guy. It ran shivers down every guy's spine in the classroom. We knew that eve-teasing is bad but before this episode, I don't think any of us had thought how disgusted a woman feels when she is eve-teased. Mathew Sir wanted us to understand exactly that. It felt horrific and also guilty to some extent because of being less sensitive to such issues before.

With many more anecdotes like these, Sir transformed the thinking processes of the students in the most logical way possible. His entire style of teaching was based on presenting hardcore raw facts, no GAS (Globally Accepted Shit in MBA Jargon). He made us question the authenticity of the innumerable systems operating around us. He only indicated the fallacies and it was for us to build our opinions based on the facts that he presented. Many of these opinions about Mathew Sir were shaped in just the first lecture. You can imagine the profoundness of his teachings throughout the entire course.

His pedagogy also involved teaching through cinema. The cinema which I am talking about is not every day Bollywood or Hollywood stuff. He showed us an entirely different world of cinema and the movies he showed left us dumbstruck. People would leave the auditorium crying and sobbing when the movies ended. For instance, the movie *Magdalene Sisters* was an Irish-British movie that presented a detailed account of the oppression faced by women in Ireland for most of the 20th century ending only in the 21st century. The storyline made it inevitable for me to think about the root cause of patriarchy in the world. I knew that patriarchy has been prevalent for ages but I was never aware of its intensity and its widespread nature even in the history of the so-called "developed countries" of today. The movie also enhanced my awareness of flaws in religion and how religion has been misused as a tool to assert power over fellow beings for personal gains or to benefit a few influential sections of society. The most beautiful part of the movie was the end which strengthens the fact that "Fear is a mere creation of the mind. If you think you are afraid of something, you are, if you don't, you aren't." The only factor stopping the ladies from escaping the asylum was a lack of courage.

The moment they let go of the fear and became audacious enough to challenge the administrative authorities, they achieved freedom and began to live the life they deserved.

The movie *The World Before Her* was a Canadian documentary film about young girls in India. It gave us meaningful insights about the world that lies in front of a young Indian woman, both from urban and rural perspectives. The movie gives mind-boggling insights into caste-based discrimination and also how important it is to understand the difference between patriotism and nationalism.

The Crucible, a Korean movie revolving around child abuse left us all shattered from within. *Grave of the Fireflies* was an animated Japanese film that displayed the tragedies of common people in Japan during World War II, through a heart-touching brother-sister relationship.

There were many more movies that focused on inequalities in society and made us realise that it is only foolish to take your blessings for granted. Getting goosebumps had become a norm while watching these movies and every one of those movies was a life-changing experience in itself. This class of cinema had always existed, but Mathew Sir is the one who gave us exposure to this and taught us its true meaning. Now, those t-shirts my seniors were wearing started making even more sense to me. Mathew Sir's course was in fact way more brilliant than all the hype surrounding it. I would insist each one of you try and attend a lecture by Mathew Sir at any place, at least once in your life.

People wonder, "Why teach such a course at a B-School?" Courses like STI and a few others from the Liberal Arts and Humanities domain tend to impart knowledge about why people behave, how they behave. They also help in building stronger human personalities. It only made me wonder why technical courses in India like Engineering, did not have courses like this. At the end of the day, education should lead to students becoming better human beings if not anything else. Mathew Sir's course and his elegant style of teaching made me realise the importance of something that I had never known was lacking in the first place. Even from a purely technical perspective, for people dealing with data or the ones designing ad campaigns, a thorough understanding of Social Sciences goes a long way in terms of improving the quality of data analytics or targeting the right audience in an ad campaign in an inclusive manner.

The course Marketing Management by Prof. Atanu Adhikari introduced us to the most dreaded "cold calls". A cold call is when a professor chooses you to answer a question irrespective of your choice to do the same. The entire course was case study based and we were supposed to read the case before every class. There were marks for class participation. Atanu Sir had supernatural powers to gauge who had read the case and who hadn't.

In case we hadn't read the case, the moment the class would start, we would all start getting goosebumps while we kept mumbling not to be called out by him in front of the class. But he could almost always smell our fear and would know whom to call out. Then we had to deal with the embarrassment of being clueless about the case study apart from the negative marks we'd end up receiving for class participation. Cold calls are any B-School student's nightmare. It helps immensely when you have friends who can explain the gist of the entire case to you 5 minutes before the class.

The most fascinating part of this course was the online simulation games. These games simulated a real-world corporate problem and we had to find an optimum solution to maximise profits by changing the variables involved, such as fixed costs, number of employees, salary level of employees (skillset dependent), operational costs, selling price, number of units manufactured, segment focus, discounts, marketing and promotional costs and many more. What made it more exciting was the fact that after every round of iteration, the game showed us how the company's performance changed by tweaking the variables, and we could perform the next iteration based on our learnings from the previous results. This was an exciting and innovative way for us to learn real-time corporate decision-making. We had access to an online simulation platform by Harvard and we were divided into groups to perform the simulation. Competition with other groups who were also trying to achieve optimum results for the company made it all the more fun.

As part of learning marketing by analysing ad campaigns, he presented Fevi-Kwik's Ad with the tagline "Todo Nahi Jodo." The ad showcased the ceremonial Wagah border parade where one soldier from India and Pakistan marches towards the centre, and the Indian soldier fixes the torn shoe of his counterpart using Fevi-Kwik in an instant. Atanu Sir made us understand that the inherent patriotism was able to successfully target the masses and the strategic timing of its rollout during an India-Pakistan cricket match made the entire country positively click with the campaign. It subtly conveyed the message that friendship and kindness triumph over hatred and animosity, a message that human beings like to relate to.

The courses just kept flowing in. There was an OB (Organisational Behaviour) course, which honestly, was more about corporate/MBA jargon than anything else. We learned two phrases, social loafer, and free rider, that eventually became our pet terms throughout the MBA. A social loafer is someone who performs less while working in a group than while working alone. A free rider is someone who does almost nothing during group assignments or projects. The best part of OB, at least for engineers, was the fact that it was very easy to get an 'A' grade just by memorising stuff. Although having to memorise is the worst form of learning, the exam formats were such that we could not do away without memorising the exact definitions. I call memorising the best thing about the course because there was so much pressure from the other courses like accounts, marketing, and microeconomics that the brain was already over-saturated. These courses involved understanding so many different concepts at the same time and applying our brains to the fullest potential during the exams. Just having to memorise stuff for a course was a welcome relief to the brain.

Term I also had the finance course which helped the engineers learn the basics of accounting. Although it was tough to learn as it was completely new for me, it still was one of the most enjoyable subjects for two reasons. First, it involved math. Second, it involved applying basic business sense, which somehow came naturally to me. I could see the implications of learning accounting and applying it to manage a company. I was spending a lot of time every day, trying to understand the basics and solving the sheets given to us by Prof. Kuntluru, our faculty for the course. I was one of the very few engineers who were able to participate in his class as much as the Commerce students did, which made his sessions all the more exciting for me. These interactions eventually led to building a great personal rapport with him. In the final exam of accounting, I solved a question for a cash-flow statement using the direct method of accounting. I made a small mistake that confused the Teaching Assistant correcting the answer sheet. Usually, the questions are solved using the indirect method of accounting and hence, my solution was a little different from the one in the marking scheme. I got 85/100. I went to Kuntluru Sir's office to explain my solution to him. He was working on his computer with the view of a heavenly valley right beside him. The natural views from the faculty offices at my IIM are beyond mesmerising. He patiently heard my appeal, eventually got convinced, and replied, "Siddharth, what you have done is correct, but the usual way to solve this is using the indirect method." I told him, "Sir, I am not from a Commerce background, so I had no idea of how it is usually solved for business purposes." He was shocked and spoke in a confused tone, "Are you kidding me? Seeing your responses in class, I could never imagine that you have not studied accounting before." I was overwhelmed with happiness, not because he changed my score to 98/100, but because I was doing things the right way. The irony was, that I had not come to an IIM to pay attention to academics, it was always about the exposure. Yet somehow, I was pursuing all the courses diligently. I was hungry to learn and the quality of some ambitious people around me was inspiring to say the least.

The first Term involved sleepless nights, running between classes, quizzes, exam preparations, "cruel" placecomm (placements' committee) sessions, sacrosanct deadlines, company pre-placement presentations, CV preparations, CV verifications, interview preparations and filling out internship application forms, all at the same time. Although CV building takes hours and hours of work, the good part is that Placecomm provides you with a standard format for building your CV. The format is designed after a lot of research and helps bring out the best in the individual. Each person has multiple CVs, based on the different verticals the individual is applying for. As an example, my finance CV was different from my marketing CV which in turn was different from my IT CV. A lot of thought goes into fine-tuning each type of CV. After all, the CV is the most important determinant of your placements.

I made a terrible mistake amidst all the hustle surrounding me. JP Morgan organises a day-long workshop to shortlist people for interviews. For its CRG (Central Research Group) role, I was shortlisted for the workshop which was supposed to begin at 8:30 am on a Sunday. I was preparing for it till late the night before. Finally, I took a cetirizine tablet before sleeping to get relief from the cold I was struggling with. The result? I didn't wake up in the morning even with the multiple alarms. I finally woke up when Manav (who later became one of my closest friends on campus) called me up at 8:35 am. I woke up, aghast, with my adrenaline gone haywire. JP Morgan was one of my dream companies and I had "almost" screwed it up for myself. I don't know how but I reached the workshop in the next 10 minutes after shaving my face and dressing up in business formals. Although it's mostly exciting to "make an entrance", this was not one of those times. I quickly looked for the seat with my name tag. I was strongly wishing to find it in one of the corners to save myself from the walk of embarrassment as the workshop had already started. But unfortunately, my seat was right in the middle of the first row. I had to walk past all the workshop instructors from JP Morgan to reach my seat.

Although I was sleep-deprived, I actively participated in the lines of questioning and gave my best to the workshop. What I learned from this experience was that pure hunger for success is your biggest motivator, which has the power to more than compensate for your other trivial mistakes. The mistake of not waking up on time was a "sunk cost". I had already made that mistake and since I could not change it, I had to make sure that it didn't negate my future results. I could still compensate for it by performing well in the workshop. The hunger for success made me do exactly that. And yes, I did make it to the final interview round for the summer placements!

The professional hard work took a toll on everyone's personal lives. A guy like me who was used to speaking to his parents for at least half an hour every day during Engineering was now speaking to them for hardly half an hour a week. My mother kept motivating me by reciting her favourite dialogue, "If you can survive and win under these circumstances, nothing in life will ever have the strength to pull you back." One needed to have the mental strength to deal with all of it at once, but in hindsight, it was more a matter of perseverance, than anything else. It was just a test of who gives up first. People had come to their heaven with so many expectations, but I wonder how many of us had imagined the struggle that was awaiting us here.

An Ode to the Professor

Academically, my favourite course of the entire MBA was also in Term I—a course called "Managerial Communication" by Prof. Anupam Das. The soft-spoken professor with a slight Bengali accent was a powerhouse of knowledge. Not just theoretical, but knowledge that guided us towards becoming better human beings. The course had topics (the specifics of which I will get into very soon) whose applications were visible in the real world, and that's the primary requirement for me to be interested in a course.

For instance, he explained to us the enhanced power of a consumer because of social media and how corporations deal with crisis/impression management, with the example of United Airlines. When a musician named David Carroll's guitar was broken during transit by United Airlines and all of his complaints/requests for claims to fix his guitar fell on deaf ears for over a year, he made a music video titled "United Breaks Guitar" that went viral on social media. Within 4 days of the video going online, United's stock fell by around 10%, costing the shareholders nearly $180 million. According to the Harvard case study, on social media, an entity's size and brand recognition made it more vulnerable to parody and attack, not safer. The crisis management team of United Airlines stepped in to save the brand image within no time. They apologized publicly, offered $1200 to replace the guitar, $1200 in flight vouchers, and donated $3000 to a music school. Their communication was mainly through their Twitter channel and focused on making things right, no matter what it took. They also mentioned that they would use the video for internal training purposes. Professor Deighton who co-authored the case study opined, "It's a transparent world. This is an environment in which you simply have to be what you say you are. You can't hope to project an idealized version of the truth."

After the Maggi ban in 2015, Maggi began its crisis management campaign titled "WeMissYouToo" showcasing the use of communication to restore its brand image. It contained a series of ads where Maggi extended gratitude towards their loyalists and responded to their messages of missing Maggi amidst the ban, with the tagline "We Miss You Too". It was about striking the chord with their consumers like a friend would do, in an endearing manner.

Anupam Sir's teachings made me realise the power of communication in its truest sense. Our frequencies matched so well, that I spent almost equal time talking to him offline as in the classroom. He pushed us to do things that we had never done before and motivated us to keep working until the results were optimum. Eventually, students ended up doing a plethora of activities that automatically boosted their all-round confidence and leadership skills. I was so moved by him that at the end of the Term, I wrote a letter of gratitude (of course after the grades were out). It's said that teaching is a thankless job, but some teachers truly deserve appreciation for the efforts they put in for the sole betterment of their students. They make a lot of effort to match frequencies with their students who are an entire generation younger than them in most cases so that they can deliver content for a better understanding of the course.

Dear Sir,

Rhetorical is the adjective that used to come to my mind while describing the Indian education system before joining the IIM. I was highly apprehensive about pursuing higher education in the country because of the degree of disbelief I had in the system. Though I have been fortunate to have had some great mentors and teachers during my school and Engineering, as all of us know, most of the people who pursue the teaching profession do it due to a lack of better options. Teaching in mainstream Indian education institutions is probably one of the few professions where there is minimal accountability for the teachers in terms of the quality of teaching. Rarely, a teacher is influential enough to bring about a positive change in the everyday life of a student. Moreover, most of the teachers simply read the day before and teach the same in the class the next day. Eventually, if they are questioned by an inquisitive mind, it is either answered through GAS, ridiculing the question, or postponement of the discussion, for obvious reasons.

At the risk of sounding like a self-obsessed individual, I would like to state that such lectures never had any learning outcome for students like me. Someone like me could comfortably understand the concepts by self-reading the books. I went to class for something which could help me in a deeper understanding of the subject. We want our teachings to enable us to relate education to the real world. To my disappointment, this hardly happened, and I only went to the classes for "attendance". At the end of every day of school or college, I used to count the number of hours I wasted in the process of the education system without getting anything in return, other than learning the social aspects of interacting with people, of course. To be frank, for a person who doesn't want to put a leash on his mind and achieve greater heights in multiple domains at the same time, it takes a lot of patience to waste so many hours every single day. After all, why was I doing all of it? Just for the mere sake of moving with the crowd, excelling in the fields that the system had senselessly designed? Very few of us have the guts to drop out of such systems and disown them completely because we have to live in a society that respects the same systems at the end of the day.

By the time I was done with engineering, my patience to deal with the system had reached a saturation point. Still, I didn't have the guts to leave a 99 percentile in CAT and hence, I joined the IIM. This proved to be a blessing in disguise. Some of the courses and professors here completely changed my outlook towards the Indian Education system. And I would proudly like to mention that your course in Managerial Communication and your pedagogy, form a part of the very few catalysts that have had the strength to influence me in a highly constructive manner. It helped to rebuild a belief in the system within me. The fact that a person who used to attend classes only to fulfill the minimum attendance criteria had 100% attendance in your course, stands as testimony to the above statement. At the end of every session, I got brilliant answers to the questions I asked myself "What did I learn from the session? Do I know something more? Will this help me in becoming a better person?" Very few people in my life have been able to do that. I have the utmost respect and gratitude towards you for the same.

In most cases, there is a huge gap between the student and the teacher. Most teachers follow "BOSSISM" and exert the power of authority over the students.

Even though they might be illogical or lack sufficient knowledge, they use their position in their favour and the student is left with no other option than to let the discussion go down the drain. It's a pure showcase of one-way communication in a place where learning cannot take place without collaborative interactions. In simple terms, such teachers DEMAND *respect, whereas teachers like you* COMMAND *respect through their pedagogy. There is a very thin line of distinction between the two, but the difference is strong enough to influence the entire education system single-handedly. There was never a need for pretence in your class. We could just be ourselves and give inputs to the discussions freely. Your opinions were never enforced on us. You played the perfect role in guiding the discussions in the right direction and leading them to a constructive conclusion. Even topics that are controversial or are considered taboo, were dealt with utter subtlety in your sessions. At times, we were even allowed to use our lingo while talking to you, but none of it ever meant that there was a lack of respect for you. Being allowed to act the way we do normally, always builds more confidence within us to have better conversations with you and gain something out of it.*

Whenever I try to think of the right pedagogy to teach a course as practical and real as Managerial Communication, I realise the intricacies involved and how difficult it is to teach such a course. I say this, on behalf of all your students, you have done an amazing job, Sir! Initiating the right kind of discussions in the class, keeping the student's attention intact, supporting them with the right kind of contemporary videos, trying to relate things to the level of our generation, along with some fun element in every class, all of this requires a massive effort, and hats off to you for implementing it flawlessly.

I had always wanted to be part of a course wherein there are practical points of reference while grading. And I was fortunate to be introduced to your course. It started with a 2-minute narration about our first two weeks of experience at the IIM campus. Those who religiously pursued the task, had the pleasure of self-analysing their communication skills after listening to their voices and on a philosophical note, digesting the eventful first few days of B-School. Next, came the task when we were asked to write a self-introduction for 500 words, with the dual purpose of preparing ourselves for placements. I can never thank you enough for making me do this as part of the course. After following your guidelines, I had almost perfected my intro and during my placement interviews, the intro came out effortlessly with the best application of the communication skills learned. Hence, the summer placement in my dream company, Silverlight. But more on that later. The strategy followed by you to make us learn the power of communication by organising a movie session of 12 Angry Men and designing a mid-term question paper along the same lines was ingenuity at its best. The atmosphere of the exam hall where we could just relax, be ourselves, listen to music, and let our thoughts flow was overwhelming in itself. Finally, the process of group presentations and the related end-term exam was an extraordinary way to make us apply the concepts in the field of marketing.

In the end, I would sincerely like to thank you for designing this course for us. I always feel that we rarely appreciate the teachers in our lives, who through their noble profession, transform us into better human beings. It was a pleasure attending your course Sir, and hence, this letter.

Opportunity Cost

Another alien course for Engineers in Term I was Microeconomics, by Prof. Shubhasis Dey. Usually dressed in formal pants and an untucked formal shirt, he was by far, the most energetic professor I have come across throughout my student life. His teaching style was full of enthusiasm and vibrant energy. His body and hands used to move in rhythm with the tone of his voice. The beauty of Shubhasis Sir's lectures lay in the fact that he always spoke about contemporary issues surrounding us. Be it the future of Apple or the stock price of Reliance, the discussions he initiated were challenging and engaging at the same time. For instance, Jio had just launched then. Shubhasis Sir gave a detailed prediction after analysing Jio's entry strategy. He predicted that with the next-generation data speeds at prices way lower than the offerings of already existing players, Jio would completely change how the telecom industry was operating in India. The low-cost schemes were not a façade and there were very less chances of Jio turning out to be a failure like Reliance Communications because of the capable leadership of Mr Mukesh Ambani and Jio's deep pockets. He also mentioned that either there would be a consolidation in the telecom industry or some big players would eventually have to exit. As we can see today, most of his predictions have come true.

Term I was the time when campaigning for the US Presidential elections, 2016 was on with full vigour. Donald Trump was getting the most media attention during those days and some of his infamous deeds were also being discussed. One day, Sir came to class and said, "I will tell you a secret. I share my birthday with Donald Trump." Just out of curiosity, the moment my lecture ended, I googled Donald Trump's birthday. I got instant Goosebumps, it was the 14th of June, the same as my birthday. I mean, what were the odds? Exact probability, 1/365 = 0.0027 ~ 0.27%. No matter if people hate or love Donald Trump, the people of the United States voted for him and he became the President of America. Now your birth date doesn't say much about you (unless you have read Malcolm Gladwell's book *Outliers*), but just a little optimism leads you to believe that you are possessed with everything you need to make it big in life. A naïve, but motivating thought, "When a person born on the same day can become the President of the USA, why can't you achieve whatever you aspire to?" It's just the simple habit of finding motivation from small incidents around you that keeps you motivated in the long run. I went to Sir the next day and told him, "Sir, as luck would have it, I also share my birthday with you and Donald Trump." He laughed and replied, "Oh God! Let's just hope he doesn't turn out to be the guy media portrays him to be in case he wins the elections."

In one of his initial lectures, Sir introduced "opportunity cost" to us. He asked how many of us had packages or job offers worth more than 10 lakhs before joining the IIM. I quickly raised my hand. He asked about the individual packages, turned out that my 13.5 lakhs was the highest CTC (Cost to Company) in the classroom that anybody had left to join the IIM. He then began the calculations, 13.5 * 2 = 27 lakhs (conservatively assuming no rise in pay over 2 years) + institute's fees of 17.5 lakhs (again, ignoring interest costs) = 44.5 lakhs. 44.5 lakhs was my opportunity cost of joining the IIM. In simpler words (not considering living costs, etc), had I not joined the IIM and taken up the job, after the two years I would have had 44.5 lakhs more with me. That was a blow! (Was I happy about my package now?) Most of us understand these calculations but still choose to go for an MBA hoping it will prove more lucrative in the long run, than the short-term opportunity cost. But the formal definition does make you rethink your choices.

One unsettling observation was the fact that this opportunity cost would have been a little lower if we weren't forced to buy textbooks during our MBA. It was included in our course fees. Although some courses needed books to be studied, for most other courses, the books were never opened. They remained sealed and cover-packed even after two years of MBA. Every year when the new batch arrives, they are welcomed with piles of fresh and useless books discarded by their seniors, lying on hostel stairways and other common areas. Some might argue that no book is useless but try paying exorbitant amounts for the books you don't need or want. The worst part, the juniors can't even reuse them! One possibility could be that the concerned professors or the college, in general, might be making money from the publishers by selling their books in huge quantities. But at whose expense? It's hard to believe that academic policymakers feel it's justified to make purchasing books mandatory unless of course there are ulterior incentives.

This highly unethical practice has been debated multiple times. But I guess few people's profits triumph over everything else, even if they have to come out of the students' pockets, over the already exorbitant MBA costs. The books should be available, but it should be a choice for the students if they want to buy the same or not. A lot of paper, student money, and campus space can be saved as students will simply borrow most of the required books from their seniors. Also, books that are not required will eventually stop being sold. It will hurt the egos of professors who have written those books but satisfying somebody's ego by spending unnecessary student money is a sin, to say the least.

Though the opportunity cost did give me motivation to work harder towards placements, it led to a lot of other questions. Opportunity costs would be different for different people. But what deserves attention is the return on investment that one can expect. The mindset of most parents in India doesn't let them take the return on investment into account. A lot of them just want a degree, no matter the cost. Talking about top schools in the country, like IIMs, although not everybody gets a decent job, most of the students manage to get good returns on their investments. But leaving the premier institutes aside, especially when you talk about private universities, the return on investment is miserable. I don't blame the universities that are charging extravagant sums of money for education. They are all smart businesspeople, in the field, to make money. They are driven by demand and supply. It just doesn't make sense to charge a lower fee when they know that parents are willing to pay higher. The need of the hour is that parents should start changing their mindsets. We need to let go of the false happiness that comes from bragging about a useless degree. Do the relatives or those nosy Aunties we like to brag in front of even matter to us in the long run? It's just an illusion a lot of us choose to live under. More than your money, it's a waste of your child's precious time and a huge opportunity cost, given the other career paths she could have followed. Choose wisely!

The Circus

In the blink of an eye, summer placements knocked at our doorsteps. The entire process turns out to be one of the cruellest (not exaggerating) experiences for a lot of people. I, fortunately, had a strong profile which got me on shortlists from all the major recruiters on campus. The moment my interviews began, I started realising the importance of the question, "Tell me about yourself." The answer to this question has the power to drive your entire interview. Use it to present your strengths, your passion, and your USPs (Unique Selling Points) in the best way possible. You just cannot give an unprepared or random answer and hope for the best. You are competing with the smartest people in the country, not being prepared is a sin in the professional world. At the same time, don't give a robotic answer. You need to mould your answer based on how the interviewer is reacting to your story. That can happen only when you combine preparation with practice. Attend as many mock interviews and group discussions as you can and use the experience of your seniors in choosing the best way forward for yourselves.

Also, try to be as honest and original with your story as you can. Most people end up offending the interviewer because a fake story indicates that you are disrespecting the interviewer's intelligence. More often than not, you will end up being trapped while trying to portray someone you are not. Apart from that, your professional etiquette (or the lack of it) will go a long way in deciding the outcome of your placements.

For me, it started with a Silverlight Investment Banking role interview. I had faced a lot of interviews even during my Engineering time, but the experience of a Silverlight interview was unmatched. It comprised 4 interview rounds for me, averaging 40 minutes each. I felt that my personality was getting polished after every round of interviews. There was a networking round before the formal interviews began. You sit with the recruiters around round tables and clear your doubts about the company's work, culture, and growth prospects. The quality of the discussions and the effectiveness of their communication only left me inspired to become a better professional.

I had prepared well for the interviews but there was one scenario that they threw at me for which I was completely unprepared. During my fourth round of interviews, the person who took my third round of interviews also came into the room and sat beside me quietly. He said, "Ignore my presence and carry on." The fourth interviewer started asking me questions and most of the questions were similar to what was asked of me in the third round of interviews. "Tell me about yourself. Why Silverlight? Why MBA? Why Finance?" Now, of course, my answers were prepared, but if I had given the same answers to the current interviewer, the previous guy would have felt that I was reciting robotic answers. If I had given different answers, he would have thought I was creating fake stories. This was something I had never faced before. The most challenging part was the fact that I did not have time to think about all this. It was all happening on the go, in real-time. I took a deep breath and finally gave answers that had the same essence as my previous answers but kept moulding my response according to the reactions of the current interviewer.

I realised it wasn't useful to throw random statements or answers just to sound good for they will question every statement that you make until they are convinced that you have thought through whatever you are saying. Right from comparing stocks in different sectors to discussing my hobbies and how I intend to make the most of my time on campus, they grilled me on every word that came out of my mouth. For instance, in my final round of interviews, I was asked, "How would you want to spend the rest of your time at the institute?" I answered that I wanted to learn professional poker with all the theories behind the game and that I wanted to read a lot about social psychology. To which, I faced a counter-question, “Poker, I understand, goes well with your overall love for math and you can probably derive analogies in the world of finance from poker, but why psychology? Any specific reason?” I was glad as I had thought through this answer, “If I understand what the other person is thinking by observing his actions which I can learn through social psychology, I would be better equipped to negotiate investment banking deals for Silverlight with the client across the table. And of course, that would also make me a better poker player.” Seeing a satisfactory smile on the interviewer’s face made me go one step ahead and say, “For instance, if I am somehow able to understand your thought process and what you expect out of me, I will be in a better position to clear this interview.” This was my final statement before leaving the interview room and the interviewer’s reaction did give me a positive vibe about how I had performed in the interview. That last statement was extempore. Good preparation had my confidence high in the interviews and helped bring out my best witty self.

After every round of interviews, we would come out only to find that more candidates had been asked to leave. Whenever the HR came towards us, we had goosebumps and an inner voice shouted, “Not me, please!” The tension in the atmosphere was crazy and the silence deafening. Finally, after 4 hours of one of the most grilling sessions in my life, three of us were called. The Head of Investment Banking greeted us with a warm smile, "Congratulations Guys! Very well deserved. Welcome to Silverlight Investment Banking." These words were music to my ears.

With the hard work I had put in during the first term and learnings from my experiences in the past, four rounds of exhausting and enriching interviews later, I managed to get into Silverlight Investment Banking, my dream role. The fact that I was an outlier as I had absolutely no finance background made it all the more special. The other two were from SRCC, Delhi University (one of the toughest colleges to get enrolled into in India), and hardcore finance students. The Silverlight interview process tested me to the core but eventually made me push my boundaries and bring out the best in me. After three months of sleepless nights, I finally went to my room and slept like a log. A sleep earned after months of toil, perseverance, and dedication toward my dreams. Proving that I could compete with the best of the best and still win, boosted my confidence in myself for undertaking any future challenges.

The process was over for me before it even began for a lot of others in the batch and I was lucky to have kept myself away from the cruelties of the process. You could derive immense learnings about human behaviour after observing the entire process. It's a process that goes on for about a week, 24 hours a day. You could see two different personalities in the majority of people.

One, before they are placed and the other, after they are placed. A lot of people who were placed were genuinely helping the others to prepare for their interviews. While the others were just faking it, trying to be there for their friends, but showing off. Then there is placement committee politics, favouritism, pressure to let go of choices, pressure on the unplaced people to sign out (the truth behind 100% placements), new friendships getting formed, old friendships getting broken, jealousy, appreciation, insecurity, gossip, bitching, the list is endless.

There are extreme situations all around. On one end, people are breaking down because of the insecurity of not getting a good job and the burden of education loans. And on the other end, people are rejoicing with their desired job roles as stars on their shoulders. A friend of mine, who was an IITian and had work experience from McKinsey did not get an internship till the end and burst into tears. And he was not alone; the summer placement process is so random that the entire aura is filled with raw emotions during that one particular week. For many students, the processes for their dream companies go on simultaneously. So, if you make it to the final round of a dream company and get rejected, you also lose out on other dream companies because you couldn't appear for them.

Some people had the best CAT percentiles, but most recruiters filtered students based on 10th, 12th, and under-graduation grades. The Institute's policy does not allow you to mention your CAT percentiles to avoid biases related to reservation. A lot of students didn't know about this before joining their dream IIM and their morale hit a new low when the companies kept releasing their shortlists and these students couldn't find their names in them. With each passing day, the pressure on the unplaced students kept growing exponentially. Since the placements happen 24 hours a day, you hardly get to sleep until you are placed. This in turn means that for a lot of students, juggling between interviews and group discussions for multiple companies simultaneously happens when they are tremendously sleep-deprived. Students are bound to screw up interviews without an active mind and the resulting guilt only makes things worse for them. Students start with defining sectors and companies of their choice, but by the end of that week, the desperation and the chaos just lead a lot of them to accept any company that would hire them. The entire process is an experience in itself. The sooner you get out of it, the better for you.

Our batch was pissed with the placement committee's favouritism and unethical practices enforced during the summer internship recruitments. For example, some of the placecommers promoted themselves and their friends to the companies' interviewing lists. The people who were already placed still had to attend group discussions and tank them to make every company believe that they were getting to choose from the best students on campus.

Some group discussions were organised in such a way that there were 6 already placed people to tank the group discussion and only one placecommer/placecommer's friend who was an actual candidate.

Such biased practices are a norm at B-Schools, mostly because only the placecommers have control of scheduling, the commoners aren't allowed to ask any questions. One notion that tries to justify this is that placecommers work hard and hence should be entitled to do things their way, so you should just accept whatever is going on and go with the flow.

So, when the scheduled placecomm re-elections were supposed to happen, the entire batch boycotted the same. Students didn't turn up to attend the session where the placecomm aspirants had to present a pitch for their candidature, after which voting happened. Previously, students agreed to everything just because they needed the best internships for themselves. Now the placecommers had no leverage, final placements were still more than a year away.

Finally, the placements' chairperson intervened and convinced the students to attend the session, ensuring that all our concerns would be addressed. The session was rescheduled and when it began, one hand after another, the entire batch started questioning the placecomm members who had upheld bossism in the summer placements' process and were now standing for re-election. There was no mercy shown, no diplomacy, no goofing around, all directly pointed and in-your-face questions. The placecommers who were guilty of misusing their position during the summer placements process were ragged on stage. They were held accountable for the smallest of their misdoings.

That day made me appreciate the quality of students who joined an IIM. Every single student was ready to take a stand for herself. They were not the ones who would allow themselves to be taken for granted. And why should they? Every single student pays a hell lot of money to join a top B-School, not getting a fair chance during placements is plain injustice. "Yes, the placecomm needs to be strict to please companies and follow their guidelines. Yes, they work day and night to get everybody in the batch placed. But seeing yourself above your batchmates and choosing to behave whichever way it pleases you, is just not acceptable", the batch sent this message that day.

The summer placements had another revelation to offer. During the entire process, be it group discussions, personal interviews or just handling processes of multiple companies simultaneously, extroverts always had an edge over introverts. This, in no way, means that extroverts are smarter, more efficient, or better leaders as compared to introverts. Some of the most successful people in the world are introverts. Both extroverts and introverts have their pros and cons. But being an extrovert does make things smoother for you at an Indian B-School. For instance, extroverts tend to network better. As most of you will agree, the quality of your professional career eventually depends on the quality of people in your network.

This prompted me to do some research with the help of some faculty members to find out what makes a person an extrovert or an introvert in the first place. There were some interesting observations. Although the major role in determining introversion is played by a person's genetic build-up, his upbringing does have a strong influence on his personality. This was further confirmed after communicating with a lot of my batchmates at the IIM, both introverts and extroverts. I tried to find commonalities and correlate how one's upbringing influences the interaction skills of a person. I found that the correlation has its roots right in the mainstream mindset of many parents. Our society makes extra efforts to establish the image of an "ideal" child. The virtual floating image of how a child should behave, sit, talk, walk, play, and interact; every aspect of a child's activity is expected to be controlled. Any child who does not adhere to these futile norms is pointed out and termed as a "naughty" kid. Of course, nobody likes to hear these words for their children. The result? The parents start running in the race of raising "ideal" kids. I am not exaggerating, just look through your childhoods and parenting happening around you. Just like the youth is imagined to be running in a rat race, parents who are bent upon raising kids as expected by society are running a rat race of their own. Many of the introverts I have met have parents who won that race.

Why do I put the word naughty within double quotes? The word "naughty" is one of the most overrated terms used for referring to children. The word is used almost casually, without giving any relevance to the actual meaning. A child is running around too much in a social gathering, "Oh, such a naughty kid." A child just poked a friend's nose with his pencil, "Stand in the corner and hold your ears, you naughty boy." A child just asked some uncomfortable questions, "She is too naughty, just doesn't keep quiet."

They are just kids, do they even understand whether what they are doing is right or wrong? Since childhood, we never fail to intermix the notions of being overactive or being inquisitive with being naughty. Most parents have this preoccupied mindset of how their child should behave in front of other people, they are intolerant towards any kind of innocent liberty the child subconsciously decides to take. Chaining down the child at every step that does not conform to the mainstream expectations eventually leads to curtailing of his public enthusiasm. The enthusiasm to talk to new people, interact with them, and get to know them, all of it soon reduces to zero. By referring to the child with a negative phrase like "naughty" again and again, you end up surrounding him with a lot of negativity. People just start perceiving him to be someone who is rebellious and does not conform to the hypothetical norms of how a person should behave.

As you age, life itself humbles you down and makes you more mature, taking care of the over-activeness. So at a broader level, genetics and environmental factors aside, a person who was highly active (mistaken to be naughty) during his childhood has more chances of becoming an extrovert because he has always been used to actively representing and engaging himself in lucrative opportunities, head-on. A person who was just asked to sit quietly and behave like an obedient (again, the mistaken definition) kid is more inclined to become an introvert, as he has never been allowed to express himself freely. Again, don't misunderstand me here. I am in no way trying to undermine the personality of an introvert. Some of the most intelligent and successful people I know are introverts. It's a personality trait, there is nothing right or wrong about it. I am just objectively trying to relate people's upbringing to the personality traits they develop and how these traits affect their networking and other social interactions.

A lot of times, we, as students or the youth, are judged instantaneously, simply because that's less effort for other people. But the ones who eventually turn out to be successful leaders are those who never surrender to these judgements and keep working to create positive and lasting impacts on their organisations and society in general.

Embracing Tranquillity

Term II entered our lives like the calm after a storm. We were so used to being busy and suddenly, we had nothing left to do. The hustle for summer placements was gone for good. The resulting peace and the serenity of my IIM's heavenly campus resulted in a beautifully tranquil environment. We finally had time for ourselves, our families, and our friends. Papa and I have always had a relationship where we make time to reflect on the eventful phases happening in our lives. Be it a family vacation, Papa's business achievements, or my career achievements, he always emphasizes chewing the cud. Until and unless we spend some time reflecting on how the events unfolded, the enjoyment or the pleasure derived from those events feels incomplete to us. Term II was finally that time.

Term I was one of the most eventful phases in my life and Term II gave me enough time to share my learnings and experiences with Papa. He had wanted to do an MBA after his Engineering but the family finances couldn't support that then. He was living the IIM journey through me. He was there, at every step, helping me make decisions and choose how to make the most of life at the IIM. Being a stockbroker, my getting into Silverlight Investment Banking was the cherry on the cake for him. He was now assured that I would get unparalleled exposure in the field of finance and was proud of the fact that I had earned it for myself.

I penned down another realisation while embracing this tranquillity. In the Bollywood Blockbuster movie 3 Idiots, Aamir Khan says this about the on-screen Suhas Tandon, "First he studied Engineering, then MBA, now working in a bank. Why did he study Engineering if he wanted to work in a bank? Such a donkey." Yes, I too am that donkey. It is so easy to get swayed by over-dramatized dialogues in Bollywood movies, but nothing can be further from the truth. Like Rancho, let me explain the flaw in the movie's dialogue with an example. There are two investment bankers, one who is a Commerce graduate and an MBA, and the other who is a computer science engineer and an MBA. A tech deal from a company like Microsoft is on the table and you are the manager of these two investment bankers. Who will you choose to be on the team? More often than not, it is better to have a person who understands the underlying products and the industry while making any deals. Moreover, whatever Commerce students learn during undergraduation is taught again during the MBA. So, after the MBA, the engineers also know the concepts taught to Commerce students during their under-graduation. But vice-versa is not true. All the knowledge you intake during your Engineering is a bonus after your MBA and knowledge never goes to waste. It's a sincere request to all readers to use utmost discretion while watching such movies. They are made for entertainment and should be dealt with likewise. I say this while being a Bollywood fanatic myself (at least I used to be) and 3 Idiots is still one of my favourite movies.

I am not suggesting that Engineering is better than Commerce in any way. It's a personal choice of the individual about what he wants to learn and is passionate about. Under-graduation, be it in any field, teaches you the technicalities of the subject while MBA teaches you the management side of things. Moreover, everybody is not sure that they would do an MBA when they have to choose the stream for undergraduation. And even when some people are sure about it, it's good to be involved in a profession that you are still passionate about, in case you don't get an MBA admission later. So, no combination is right or wrong, irrespective of what job you take after your MBA.

It was also in Term II that I was first introduced to the world of poker. Exposure to poker is inevitable at B-Schools because of the analogies between poker and corporate strategies. One of my closest friends, Vikas

Agarwal helped me learn the tricks of the trade. The tall, dark (although he prefers wheatish), flamboyant personality was so witty that playing good poker came naturally to him. He was a few years older than me and had been playing professional poker for a long time now.

Soon, we formed a group of 6 hardcore poker enthusiasts, called the PCG (Poker Core Group). The group consisted of Vikas, Ranka, Patle, Gagan, Bala, and SidJ (my moniker). Ranka is one of the wittiest people I know and a poker player whose strategies just leave you dumbstruck. You go broke playing against him, and you don't even realise what hit you. As I am writing this book, Ranka is minting money playing online poker and live international tournaments. Patle was the best sportsperson on campus and the most logical guy on the poker table, although his gambling instincts got the better of him at times. Apart from that, Patle has spent hours and hours helping me edit this book, he is just the friend you can always count on. Gagan and Bala were doing their PhD at the IIM and were quite senior to us. Every 2-hour poker session had a follow-up session between me and Vikas which lasted for a minimum of 30 minutes. This is where I was reflecting on the mistakes I made, the opportunities I missed, and the strategies that I should have followed. And Vikas was the perfect coach.

He was one of the only 3 CAs (Chartered Accountants) in the batch and was known as the Fin (Finance) God because of his deep-rooted knowledge of the world of finance. People join IIMs to get into investment banking, he had left niche investment banking jobs to join an IIM. During Term I, he was the go-to guy for me to clear all my finance-related doubts and to help me prepare for placements. He was also the first person I informed about my Silverlight internship offer along with expressing immense gratitude towards him. He was filled with pride up to his height.

A fun fact, even Vikas and I share the same birthday and we came to know about this long after we had already realised that we showcased uncanny similarities. In Term II, the finance sessions I earlier had with him turned into poker sessions. Because of the matching frequencies, we also spent a lot of time talking about philosophy, people, and life in general. Vikas is by far one of the smartest people I have ever met.

To increase my poker proficiency, I started reading Doyle Brunson's book Super System on Poker. Doyle Brunson is one of the most revered poker legends of all time. People who understand poker know that it is a game of skill and not gambling. So, it is of utmost importance that one keeps learning poker through multiple sources to understand different perceptions as well as different aspects of the game. The involvement of human psychology and people-reading makes it all the more interesting. I also started watching the World Series of Poker videos on YouTube. Eventually, I was contributing a good amount of my day towards learning and playing poker.

By now I had also learned that a single-minded focus is one of the most important criteria to develop specific skill sets or achieve your short and long-term goals. Be it Android App-Development, recruiting for my start-up in my Engineering college, or getting into an IIM, all of these were results of a single-minded focus and sheer dedication.

But what about my academics? How did I manage time? I could do all of this because of Chirag Kansal, one of my other closest friends on campus. I have never seen a person who imbibes "Simple living and high thinking" better than Chirag. He used to selflessly help me with my exam preparations at the eleventh hour and guide me on how to go about doing assignments and group projects during the normal course of events. His hard work and sincerity could only leave every individual around him inspired. I honestly wonder what mess I would have been in, had it not been for Chirag.

In hindsight, I realise that Term II was more about getting to know people and forming everlasting friendships. Taking advantage of the resort-like beauty of the campus, we formed a group of 6-7 people and started going on late-night walks. The main gate of the campus is 2 km downhill from the hostel area. We used to walk the entire course up and down amidst the lush green forest-like surroundings. The symphony of fresh air and the friendly banter were the perfect accompaniments. This walking group, jokingly called the "Night Walkers" soon became some of the closest friendships that were formed on campus. Arpita, who's now my wife, Chirag (Chiru), Gaurav (GJ), Shailza (Telly), Shobhit (Mittal), and I, were the permanent ones in the group with several others who kept coming and going.

Apart from partying and chilling, Term II had some really interesting academic courses. There is one professor who deserves a mention when I think about my learning from the institute: Prof. G. Anand, who taught us Operations Management-1. Out of the entire course, what I remember the most vividly is his very first lecture. The topic was a case study of Indigo Airlines, on how it managed to beat the competition and survive when most other airlines nosedived. I was never an operations guy, always interested more in other subjects, but the way he presented the case was mind-boggling.

- 2006: Commenced operations under InterGlobe Enterprises Pvt. Ltd.
- 38 domestic and 5 international destinations with close to 647 daily flights
- Sept-2011: Commenced international operations; viz. Delhi / Mumbai to Muscat, Kathmandu, Dubai, Singapore and Bangkok
- Has Grown at a steady clip: addition of eight planes every year

- Market leader—39.8% market share as of Jul 2016
- India's youngest airline, having flown over 20 million passengers

Indigo's competitive priorities:

- On time delivery
- Low cost
- Hassle-free services
- Value-added services
- Clean and fresh (Hygienic)
- Q-Busters
- Step less stairs or ramps

One of the major Unique Selling Points of Indigo was its low cost and that could only be achieved with lower operational costs. Indigo reduces these costs broadly divided into the following 2 categories, Infrastructure:

- Same type of flights - 90 Airbus A320 (approx.). This leads to a huge reduction in hiring, training, maintenance and upgradation costs
- Base in Delhi
- Serving tier-2 cities - typically short-haul flights
- Lean crew or no. of persons required per flight is less (96 people per flight in comparison to 250 for Air India)
- Highest number of CAT III-trained pilots

- Single passenger class and hence no differential entry or treatment (standardisation)
- Lightweight seats - Improved fuel efficiency
- More number of seats - More occupancy and more revenue
- High utilisation of aircraft with minimum layovers (12 hours per plane per day)

Planning and Control

- Boarding gate closes 30 mins (they mean it)
- Mostly point-to-point flights
- Quick turnaround of flights - with minimal items within the flight
- No free food or in-flight entertainment
- No-frill boarding area and transfer buses
- Minimal advertisements on tickets, buses, etc., but not in inflight magazines
- Alliance with Airbus for effective maintenance
- Lowest attrition of people and good culture
- Employees do take up multiple roles (Ground Staff)

Initially, it was hard to make sense of the facts, but when the class ended, I realised how brilliantly Sir had opened up the entire case in a single lecture. I could never imagine teaching a highly technical case with such wholesome efficiency. One step at a time, he kept unfolding different aspects of the case and all of them finally contributed to the increased bottom line (net profit) of Indigo Airlines. Anand Sir taught me the actual meaning and importance of a live case study. I could never become an expert in that subject, but I will always remember the learnings from that Indigo Airlines case. I wish our education system had more professors like him as education is only meaningful when you can implement the learning in real life. Unfortunately, our education system is far from it. Mostly the pedagogy involves memorising stuff to clear the next day's exams and then forgetting everything right after. Moreover, our education system does not teach us anything related to the management of money or finances in general, which is one of the most practical considerations in the real world.

Talking about education relevant to the real world would be incomplete without talking about the Business Ethics course. It was arguably one of the most impactful courses throughout the entire two years of my MBA. This course was conducted by Prof. Lionel Aranha, one of the most loved professors across different colleges in India. He was a guest faculty at our campus and also taught at another premier IIM. He introduced a different side of the corporate world to us. The ruthless steps taken by some of the corporate giants worldwide to increase their profitability and why they do not lead to a better world in the long run, were the essence of his lectures. His pedagogy focused on learning from movies based on the unethical activities of corporations and deriving other real-life analogies around us. We were motivated to create presentations on those movies and give suggestions on how some catastrophic events could have been avoided or can be avoided in the future. It forced us to think beyond profits and towards the overall advancement of humankind.

Sir has a unique way of presenting his case. No floating around, only facts. I have hardly come across a person who has the calibre of teaching ethics the way Lionel Sir does. I somehow always linked his personality to that of Morgan Freeman, probably because of his communication skills. He was straightforward, calm, bold, and effective, all at the same time. Sir's series of #JustSaying posts on Facebook and Instagram are the biggest eye-openers. I can never thank him enough for opening my mind to look at the same thing from multiple angles. He was great friends with Mathew Sir. When students at IIM Indore used to praise him, he used to reply, "I am just a teacher, Mathew is GOD." It's priceless exposure that one gets from such professors, who travel and research extensively to impart the best of knowledge from all spheres of existence. These courses teach life to us and are more important than the technical stuff which is always given more importance by a preoccupied mind. I wish I had such courses back in high school.

Amidst all this, now that I look back, there is one major mistake that I committed during this period. I let myself get complacent after achieving the dream internship offer from Silverlight. I had forgotten about my entrepreneurial dreams or about getting involved in the family business. I knew I wanted to settle down in business eventually. This resulted in a mindset that I would work for a year or two, gain some exposure, and return to business, either the family business or a new entrepreneurial venture. But I had become a victim of procrastination. Even though my long-term goals were crystal clear, I never thought of starting to work on business projects during college. I had ample time and I wasted it. I let the privileges of being an IIM student and the last few years of college enjoyment get to my head. I was just satisfied with my internship offer and was also prepared to work hard enough to convert it into a Pre-Placement Offer (PPO). A PPO is a job offer that is made to the candidate based on her internship performance. Such candidates need not sit for interviews again during the final placements.

The sad part? I had stopped looking at the bigger picture. I had so much time to experiment with new business ideas and get them validated by the best of professors, but again, I wasted it. The environment at an IIM is such that almost everybody is placement-oriented and it's only practical to be like that because of the giant education loan. My mistake was that even though I had joined the IIM for reasons other than placements, I had stopped working as hard towards my business plans as I was working before the IIM.

Breaking Point

Remember how I told you that Term II was the calm after a storm? But who would have thought that the calm after a storm could also be the calm before another storm? The calm after a storm in my professional life turned out to be the calm before a storm in my personal life. This storm was fierce, and unforeseen, and caught me and my entire family completely off guard.

Everything was going smoothly, until one ghastly day, Papa was diagnosed with cancer. Cancer is something that you only hear about, accepting that it has found its way into one of your own is one of the toughest realities to deal with. At the end of December 2016, just a few days before Term III was supposed to begin, Papa contracted jaundice. On 3rd January 2017, I left for college as the family took papa to Delhi for treatment. On further diagnosis, it was revealed that Papa had a tumour in the bile duct, which was causing "obstructive jaundice". Whether or not that tumour was malignant was yet to be ascertained, but by doctors' past experiences, such tumours mostly turned out to be malignant. Since the tumour was localised, surgery was possible and was scheduled for a few days later. He was supposed to undergo Whipple's Surgery - one of the most complicated and rare surgeries to be performed, as it involves the removal of the head of the pancreas, the first part of the small intestine, the gallbladder, the bile duct, and a part of the stomach. I was never told about the name or the complications of the surgery until many days later. All I knew was that it was a normal surgery in which the tumour was removed. My family (a Joint family with 2 uncles and their immediate families) had told me that it was not a serious situation and I should not leave college to join my mother and uncles in the hospital. Papa had strictly told everyone not to tell me the details because he was afraid that I would leave everything and run to the hospital and spoil my career, which he could not live with.

The biopsy of the tumour removed from the body later revealed that it was malignant. Post the surgery, it was a good twenty days before he was discharged from the hospital, and my mother reluctantly told me the details of the procedure. It was dreadful to imagine what Papa had undergone in the last few days. I had yet to come to terms with Papa's cancer diagnosis, and understanding the specific details of what Papa had gone through only made things worse for me. The only consoling factor was that it was finally over.

The doctors said that he was cancer-free but would have to take preventive chemotherapy until June. He was back home, ready to regain all his health with his positive mindset. Three to four days after Papa reached home, I flew to Bhilai for a weekend trip to meet him. When I reached home in the evening, Papa was sleeping in his bedroom. He had become weak like a stick. I couldn't stand looking at his condition. Maa consoled me and explained to me how tough the last few days had been and how Papa had been in an even worse condition before.

When Papa woke up, he gave me a hug with a smile on his face, as if nothing had happened. At that very moment, I realised how strong fathers are. They never show their true emotions, they only meet you with a smile so you can smile back. Since that day, Papa has become my ultimate hero.

Maa, my grandma, and every other family member were taking care of Papa in some way or the other. It had become everyone's life goal to bring Papa back to his previous healthy self. Since he had to take preventive chemotherapy, it was hard for Papa to regain health quickly. But everyone was fighting for him. One of my uncles was managing the family business and the other uncle would take Papa for chemotherapy along with Maa. Papa's journey while fighting cancer made me realise the importance of family even more. Had it not been for the support of my uncles, aunts, and the entire family, I would have had to drop out of my MBA. They made sure that Papa was getting the best treatment available without letting my career and the family get affected.

The worst was over. I was back on campus for my Term III. My mind was half occupied with Papa's treatment and I had to make sure that I did not let it have any drastic effect on my MBA. I rarely used to discuss anything about Papa's treatment with my friends at college. My mother had taught me very early in life that sympathy can never be your friend. While sympathy feels good at the moment, in the long run, it makes you weak internally. It reduces your strength in dealing with situations and affects your logical thinking abilities. But, fighting all alone does have its associated costs. It takes a toll on your mental health as what is going on in your mind is different from what you express in front of others. Whatever it is, you get used to it.

Tricks of the Trade

Head Start to Term III was a road trip covering a good portion of Kerala with a group of friends to explore God's own country and release the stress off my mind.

I also knew that I had been quite lackadaisical during Term II. My hard work during Term I rewarded me with my dream Silverlight internship, now the focus was on getting it converted into a PPO. I had to revisit the concepts of finance thoroughly and prepare for any challenge that could be thrown at me. Honestly, I am a typical procrastinator and to fight that, I have devised a strategy that works for me every time. Whenever I want to achieve something, I say it out loud to the people around me. That invariably puts pressure on me to fulfil whatever I had claimed or face humiliation at the hands of others. The fear of failure does wonders when it comes to achieving your goals.

During my Engineering days, I wanted to recruit for my start-up at my own campus. It was a big ambition for me as nobody had recruited in my college before while still being a student at the same college. It involved a lot of courage in terms of the organising process, convincing the college authorities that it was a genuine internship offer, convincing the students to apply for it, and arranging the money to offer as a stipend. I didn't even know how to create a decent PowerPoint presentation, let alone conduct recruitment.

At the beginning of the final year, I told almost everyone in the batch that I would conduct recruitment before graduating. With my dad's and his research team's guidance, I carefully invested money in the stock markets and made enough to take care of the stipends that I had to offer. I registered a private limited company to convince the college of the authenticity of the internship offering. To convince students to apply for the summer internship, I drafted a highly professional email after taking cues from the other well-established MNCs' emails that offered internships on campus. To organise the process better, I requested the best coders in my batch to help me with the interviews. Everything fell into place. It was just about the right kind of motivation. The result: there was a hall full of students gathered for interviews on a Saturday morning. Along with that, the Dean's farewell speech began with appreciating my team for creating history in PESIT by conducting recruitments on campus even before graduating.

So, this time, I repeated exactly that. I told my friends that I would get a PPO from Silverlight, no matter how harsh the working hours were. When you say it out loud, it starts growing onto you and automatically beats the negative effects of procrastination. But there is a lot of caution that needs to be exercised while adopting this strategy. The strategy is quite vulnerable as it can lead to a lot of mental stress that the fear of failure brings along with it. So, it should not be replicated in a generalised manner. It only works if you can channel your energy in the right direction and use the fear of failure as a motivation to work hard.

The weaknesses don't necessarily have to pull you back. It's not that successful people don't have weaknesses. What makes them successful is the fact that they are aware of their weaknesses and they play to their strengths while devising strategies to minimise the impact of these weaknesses. The first step in tackling a weakness is essentially becoming aware of it, which most of us fail to do.

Term III also involved a lot of poker again, which led to sleepless nights. One weekend, the entire PCG gang planned a poker cum relaxation trip to Wayanad, a stunning hill station in Kerala. We reached the jungle homestay Saturday morning and it was raining cats and dogs. We started a poker session and owing to the thrill seekers within us, eventually decided that we wouldn't stop playing until it stopped raining. Who had imagined that the rain gods were determined to test our poker obedience for the next 48 hours straight? The rains just didn't stop and since we were committed to our word, we didn't stop either. We planned a schedule such that only one out of the 6 of us was allowed to sleep at any given point in time and nobody would sleep for more than 4 hours at a stretch. Since the homestay had minimal resources, we lived on Maggi, chips, water, and tea for 2 days and 2 nights. By Monday morning, we had become zombies, who couldn't process any thought other than poker. The rains still hadn't stopped but it was time to return to college and attend the morning lecture. I hadn't played poker for this long ever; the learnings were immense. Poker tests your patience, tests if you can let go of your ego for the larger monetary incentive, teaches you bankroll management, tests your pattern observation and people reading skills, improves your speech play and negotiation skills, teaches you to keep changing gears in your strategy in the short-term to achieve the greater goal in the long-term, teaches you to deal with vulnerability and holds you accountable for every move you make. More than anything else it prepares you for the fact that even when you do everything right, a tiny amount of bad luck can still screw you and can screw you big. You have to be prepared to face it with a smile (or a poker face if you will) and move on. The more I played poker, the more I realised that poker resembles the game of life in a myriad of ways.

We directly went to attend the morning lecture on reaching college and the challenge staring at us was to stay awake. I had a trick that was "almost" foolproof when it came to sleeping in class while escaping the attention of the professors. I had trained myself to keep nodding my head from time to time while sleeping during the lecture. This was in synchronised motion with the rocking of my chair. I had two other things in my favour: one, my black-rimmed spectacles that made it hard for my eyes to be visible, and two, my "saviour", Stuti Gupta, who used to sit beside me. Whenever a professor was doubtful about my attention, Stuti used to kick me on my leg and wake me up. I had trained my mind such that when this happened, I used to open my eyes along with the sideways nodding of my head to make it appear that I was concentrating on something.

Now about that "almost" foolproof bit. Well, that's because it gets a little too risky at times. In the morning lecture right after the weekend poker saga, Prof. Leena, who taught Macroeconomics to us, became doubtful of my attention and asked me a question randomly. I was in deep sleep and on top of that, I was dreaming about playing a full-fledged hand on a poker table during my sleep. In the dream, Ranka had gone all-in and I was just about to call his bluff. Suddenly, Stuti kicked me and I woke up, aghast. The game was over (both metaphorically and literally). It took me a good 10 seconds to realise where I was. There was silence all around and Leena Ma'am was looking at me. I had guessed that she had asked me a question. I instantly recalled Baba Rancho's teachings from *3 Idiots*, took a deep breath, and told myself, "AAL IS WELL, AAL IS WELL." Hesitantly, I asked Ma'am if she could repeat the question. Being the polite professor that she was, she repeated the question. It was a yes/ no question, but I had no idea of the answer. Any answer had a 50% probability of being right. I pulled my senses together and while trying to gauge the answer from the tone of her question, put my bets on "No". It was a complete fluke, but it was right! I thanked my stars and Stuti. The entire class burst into laughter as everybody was aware of this little trick of mine. I was just trying to keep my calm and not burst into laughter myself. I think Prof. Leena also understood what was going on, but she was kind enough to let it go.

This was not the end of this trick. There was an HRM (Human Resource Management) lecture going on. Prof. Krishnan had assigned a group activity where one person was supposed to teach something new to the other members of the group. I taught my group how to sleep without getting caught. It was okay till here, but after the activity, Prof. Krishnan asked us to narrate our experiences to everybody. Everybody started pushing me to teach the entire class my little trick of sleeping. Finally, I volunteered but made Krishnan Sir promise me something before. I said, "Sir, I am going to teach everyone how to sleep in a lecture without getting caught, but you have to promise me that you won't use it against me." Prof. Krishnan, being the sport he was, promised me that in his jolly tone. This was followed by my sleeping on my chair while nodding my head along with synchronised rocking of my chair and Stuti suddenly waking me up. It was hysterical. Such beautiful days, I guess this is why people say, "You never get the fun of college days back in life." And I am filled with nostalgia even while writing this. The beauty of these memories is that they involve times of pure happiness, unbridled energy, and hope for a better future.

Term III was also the term when hostel room allocation for the 2nd year took place. Unfortunately, Vikas and I ended up with a room that was devoid of campus's heavenly valley view and was a little closer to the common washrooms. Things turned interesting when we figured out that the guys with the best room, Bansal and Meena, were poker enthusiasts and used to consider themselves great poker players. We knew what to do next. Vikas and I challenged them to Heads Up (meaning only 2 players playing a poker game on the table) poker matches.

The bet was that if we won, we would get that beautiful valley view room. What was the incentive for Bansal and Meena? Well, Vikas and I had together bought a second-hand Pulsar 220 bike, costing around ₹54,000. If we lost, we offered that the bike would be theirs and they could also of course keep their room.

The bet was on. While I had studied the game deeply, Vikas had a vast life experience in terms of hours spent on a poker table after having played in various casinos. This made us a potent combo of skills backed by education and experience. We still chose to keep a low profile about how much we knew about poker. In addition to that, through some other common friends, we convinced Bansal and Meena that they were the favourites to win the game which made them a little less guarded and a little more relaxed.

One Saturday night, the games began around 10 pm, with 2 poker tables, 2 Heads-Up matches, and some close spectators from both sides. We started with 50 BBs (Big Blinds) each and if anybody lost all the chips in between, he could reload for 50 BBs. The reloads would stop at 2:00 am. After that, the game would end when one player was able to win all the chips of his opponent. If the two winning players were from opposite teams, their final chip stacks would be counted. If the final chip stacks were also equal, all bets would be cancelled, back to the status quo.

Vikas and I played some of the best poker of our lives that night. We 'played the man', we applied GTO (Game Theory Optimal), we made them win when we wanted to and took advantage of it later, we maximised the profits when we had the best hands and minimised the losses when we had the second best. We knew we were better players but we didn't let it get to our heads, we worked hard to win. Also, those guys were better than we had expected them to be.

By 3:15 am, Vikas had eliminated Meena. Bansal and I were still playing. We were both deep-stacked, Bansal had 275 BBs and I had 325 BBs. The last hand was a breeze, so to speak. Bansal was on the button and hence, the first to act. In heads-up games, the one with the dealer button is the first to act pre-flop. He opened with 3 BBs. This was his standard raise. I looked at my cards and found a suited AK in my den. I was filled with confidence. I usually played AK like one plays Aces. I 3-bet him with 9 BBs and expected him to flat call (he had become pretty loose towards the end). However, he 4-bet me with 27 BBs. Although I had a 36% probability of hitting an Ace or King on the flop (along with additional implied odds), I was a bit nervous as I remembered what Vikas had once told me about AK, "Do you know that AK is also known as the big slick? It refers to some destructive oil spill that had happened in the US and serves as a reminder as to how sometimes it can be destructive for the player holding the hand."

I thought about 5-betting the hand but that would have meant committing close to 30-40% of my stack, which I didn't want to do because Bansal was the kind of guy who'd call with 44 and put me in a spot post-flop because he'd be in position. So, I decided to flat the hand and then take it from there.

Flop was 9(s) Q(d) A(h) (s-spades, d-diamonds, h-hearts, c-clubs). I had flopped the top pair and felt slightly at ease and decided to check it to him. He bet half the pot. Man, I was a bit nervous now, "Why didn't

I 5-bet pre-flop and then fold if he shoved? I could have still saved some money. How do I fold this hand? He could have so many combos that dominate me. But after this flop, I don't think I can go anywhere." So, I called.

The turn was K(d). The board looked slightly better: 9(s) Q(d) A(h) K(d). I had turned 2 pairs and was now better than many of the combos he could have had. The pot had inflated to 108 BBs. I checked again and he bet slightly less this time, around 35 BBs. This seemed fishy. This could either be him having a solid hand or him thinking that I had a really solid hand. And then, his eyes looked at me trying to show that he wasn't scared one bit, as if he had a very strong hand. But at the same time, he scratched his neck with his thumb, that was his tell. He did that whenever he was on a mediocre hand. I flat-called again to make him believe that his stare had convinced me of his strong hand. The pot was now 178 BBs.

The river was the money card, an Ace of clubs. 9(s) Q(d) A(h) K(d) A(c). With this, I had turned Aces full of Kings and all of my nervousness evaporated. Of course, I pretended like I had just been slapped by my high-school crush, to convince him that the river was really bad for me.

Now, I could hear the Mortal Kombat game sound bite that played at the end of a fight sequence with the bright red stylized font: "FINISH HIM." So, I decided to think a bit more. He had been trying to narrate the story of a very strong hand all this while. The only way to make him commit "hara-kiri" was by giving him further evidence of my weakness.

So, on the river, I led out with just 1/5th of the pot, trying to showcase that my fear had gotten the better of me and that I didn't know how to react. The total pot size with this bet became around 220 BBs. He waited for 10 seconds and then I saw a wicked smile on his face with which he pushed his stack all in. He was slightly taken aback by seeing my instant call. He showed AJ with his trips. Vikas had been observing the hand all along and tried to guess my hand in the *Chak De India* SRK way before I opened my cards, "SJ has Pocket Queens, actually no because he would have 5-bet pre-flop with them. He probably has 10 J making a straight for him but SJ would have tried to semi-bluff his open-ender on the flop and re-raised on the turn, so that is also out. Oh Yes! SJ, show me the BIG SLICK, COME ON (he has his unique way of saying this)!" I opened my cards and said, "That's how it's done!", with a mic-drop gesture.

Although Bansal did not have a hand as strong as Matt Damon's final losing hand from the first scene of the masterpiece movie *Rounders*, he sure had that look of losing big. We had won, both of us. We could finally get rid of the sad room and the occasional whiff of shit from the washrooms. The bike was also ours to keep.

There was a strange takeaway from that night though. Even though it was a highly competitive and cut-throat session, we enjoyed it thoroughly. We ended up forming strong friendships with Bansal and Meena, who later went on to become our poker buddies. A lot of poker knowledge started flowing both ways and occasional poker sessions became a norm with them. We never gave them a chance to win their room back though!

Academically, after a plethora of quizzes, projects, presentations, assignments, and exams, Term III finally came to an end. Although we were accustomed to managing stress and multitasking by now, in terms of academics, this had been the most exhausting Term. In hindsight, I realise multiple techniques could be used to deal with the crazy schedule.

One, respect deadlines. It is always better to plan your calendar at least one day in advance. By keeping up with the deadlines, you automatically find yourself in a position where you are comfortable with multiple things going around at the same time.

Two, prioritise. You cannot do everything with the same optimum results at the same time. Prioritise tasks where you want to focus more of your energy or where the risk-reward ratio is in your favour. The people involved in clubs/committees prioritise their extra-curricular work and most of them happily take a hit on their grades. The people in the race for top academic positions and scholarships based on grades prioritise academics over anything else and are happy being less social, in general. Nothing right or wrong about it. It's about choosing what you want for yourself, but you have to do justice to whatever you choose to prioritise.

Third, don't procrastinate. This, in turn, compliments the first point of respecting deadlines. You start with postponing one task, then keep adding to the pile and finally, the pile becomes as huge as the number of clothes on your helpless hostel room chair. Eventually, you lose the motivation to execute even one of these tasks.

Fourth, pay attention in the classes (well, most of them). The good thing about academics is that at the top IIMs, most of the courses are designed keeping in mind the industry requirements. It's not very hard to understand the real-life significance of the concepts taught, which makes it interesting. If you make that little extra effort to be attentive during lectures, you will save a lot of time while preparing for quizzes or exams.

Fifth, keep the faith alive. You need to have that confidence of being able to sail through all the challenges.

It's not like I followed all the above five points, but by the end of the first year, I had realised that this is how it should have been done. There is also a sixth point, which I executed pretty well and is also my personal favourite, although it is a little unorthodox. Use your relationships effectively. In most cases, you have a choice to form your groups while doing projects/assignments. Form groups with people whom you can rely on and who understand the meaning of true friendship. It is great to be a part of a team where everyone is ready to cover for one another. Everyone will have both good and bad days, it boosts your morale when you know your friends have your back on a bad day. Of course, nobody can do the work for you, but you can improve your efficiency by helping each other so that everyone doesn't have to start the task from scratch. The feeling of having a group that you can trust and fall back on is something that makes your life at an IIM all the more animated. It gives you the strength to take on new challenges. Please don't confuse this with networking. A network is way more professional and formal. I am talking about a group of friends, people you want to be with without any specific reasons. I feel that this is the most important treasure you take out of your B-School life. Networks can be formed by a lot of people, but these treasures are found by only a few blessed and lucky ones.

What followed made the brutal Term III look like a mere fun ride in Disney World. Yes, the Internship. In terms of professional growth/advancement, the two months of Internship were probably the most crucial months of my career. The internship tested me, grilled me, and motivated me, but most important of all, it pushed my boundaries.

The Internship

"If you are the smartest person in the room, change the room." If you enjoy being the smartest person in the room and are reluctant to challenge yourself, you are losing out on the opportunity to grow as an individual. You need to be surrounded by people who are smarter than you in some way or the other, only then you can gift yourself the pleasure of continuous learning. This is the philosophy that has always kept me motivated. I kept changing my room until I reached Silverlight that too, the Investment Banking Division.

Every single person on the floor appeared to be the smartest of people I had ever met. It took me some time to digest the fact that now, I was a part of this group too. My father had prepared me to not let this feeling get into my head. Reaching a place like this is the ultimate "heaven" for a lot of finance enthusiasts like me. This leaves a lot of scope for an individual to start taking things for granted, to just sit back and relish the achievements. If not respected, the same heaven would start feeling like hell in no time. It is hard to reach the top, but what my experiences have taught me is that it is harder to stay at the top than to reach there. I was blessed with the rarest of opportunities and I had to make sure that I proved myself worthy of them. Since I joined the IIM as a fresher, I did not have too many expectations from the internship. But Silverlight made sure that my experience was beyond anything that I could have expected. Let's just say that I was thirsty and I was fed water from a fire hose. No matter the force of the water gushing out of that pipe, the people around me made sure that I was using every drop of it to quench my thirst. It was ingrained in their culture to work collectively and help the interns, irrespective of the silliness of our questions. This is where I learned the definition and significance of the term "culture" at an MNC. It used to sound like a highly overrated and overused term to me when I kept hearing about it during Pre-Placement Company Presentations back in college. At Silverlight, all the interns were welcomed with open arms. We weren't expected to be a bunch of know-it-all's. The only expectation Silverlight had from us was that we showed a willingness and eagerness to learn. We could go to any individual on the floor, no matter whether the person was an Analyst, Associate, or VP (Vice President), and request his/her advice without any inhibitions. Every person was there to guide us, selflessly, without any judgement. The politeness in their communication, the professionalism in dealing with issues, and the clarity of thought while working on projects just kept inspiring me to become a better person, both professionally and personally.

The best part was that these people knew how to have fun and enjoy life while managing work at the same time. That is the kind of people I had always loved to be around. To live a joyous life, you can't afford to waste time around people who are just workaholics without any respect for personal happiness. At the same time, it's foolish to be around people who are just chilling in life, because they can never motivate you to grow further. At the end of the day, your mindset is a blend of the mindsets of the people you end up spending most of your time with.

I was assigned to the ANZ (Australia New Zealand) team. I couldn't thank my stars more. My team had Ishu and Leah, two of the most loved and respected people on the floor. The quality of learning with these people was a blessing that came quite early in my career. There was Akhilesh, my senior from PESIT, who made sure I learned something new every day. He was my go-to person, be it any kind of advice, work or career-related.

The beauty of the internship's structure was that we had opportunities to interact with and learn from almost everybody on the floor as part of the process itself. In hindsight, I realise that it was the perfect way to network with so many people in such a short period. There was knowledge and wisdom all around. I enthusiastically looked forward to the intellectually stimulating conversations with these people every morning. All the interns were learning to manage stress, deal with deadlines and polish their personalities all at the same time. Also, it was of utmost importance that we prioritised our tasks. We were given work from all directions and all with short deadlines. The challenge lay in the fact that we didn't even have enough time to prioritise work. We struggled a lot initially but soon prioritising became a habit and we started doing it subconsciously. Without prioritising, there was no way forward. Everything had to be done, but one bottleneck could make all the other scheduled tasks go haywire. Real-time decision-making, changing priorities depending on how external circumstances change and eventually delivering the best for every task are some of the techniques that helped us sail through the Internship.

Initially, we were hesitant to convey our existing workload to the person allocating the next task to us. But with time, we realised it's important to understand how much work we already have on our plates and commit to new tasks accordingly. The last thing you want is to take up a new task and not be able to deliver the desired results. There is nothing more demoralising than substandard work at a place like Silverlight and over-commitment is a highly unprofessional trait. Having said that, I would strongly advise people who pursue similar internships in the future to focus not just on work, but also on building relationships. When your manager wants to take you out for lunch, or a teammate wants to go for a walk, or a colleague wants to share a short break, say "Yes" to them. Maybe cut it short if you are overloaded with work but do spend time building personal relationships. Today, when I look back, I remember those walks, lunches, and short breaks more than I remember the actual tasks that I was working on. The memories are priceless and those short twenty minutes can go a long way in building strong relationships for the future. We are all humans at the end of the day. The 90-hour weeks at an investment banking company can take a toll on your brain if you just keep working without any informal interactions. You need to find ways to relax your saturated mind while working. If not anything else, personal connections with others at a workplace are what differentiates a human from a robot.

The most transformative moments at Silverlight were the Mid-Evaluation and Final-Evaluation which consisted of giving a presentation about our pitchbooks. It was a perfect boardroom experience and we had to pitch our ideas to the senior management of Silverlight. It was as real as it could get. Along with the stress of delivering your pitch right, there was a lot of fun surrounding the presentations. The quality of the questions asked was mind-blowing. I felt like I was growing as an individual, just by being in that room. There were some horrible mistakes that I made as well. Ajay a VP at Silverlight, asked me, "What is the margin in x segment of the company you are pitching?" I had no idea about it. I replied, "The margin is not relevant here, we are focusing on the multi-fold growth rate of this segment." The counter question, "That's all right, but what is the margin anyway?" Then came my epic reply, "It's not too high and it's not too low, and hence, we didn't focus on the margin." The entire panel was laughing and I somehow managed to control my laughter. Though a little smile on my face indicated that I knew I was bullshitting. I hurriedly moved on to the next slide to avoid making a fool out of myself even further. But this was far from over. Ajay caught hold of me in a "Networking Meet" a few days later and asked, "You were the one, right? Not too high not too low?" I dodged the question with a stupid laugh and prayed that he just enjoyed his beer and got away from the topic, but he gave me a brilliant suggestion instead. On a lighter note, he suggested, "The correct answer to such questions is always a 13.42% (or any random number) margin. You can't get away with it every time, but more often than not, you can convince the other person if your answer is in a believable range and you say it with confidence." Gyaan of the day!

The internship was full of such mistakes, but each mistake presented a learning opportunity that made us better for the future. It taught us the nuances of making a successful corporate career and channelling our competitive spirit into productivity at work. It taught us that although there is no substitute for hard work, it can only triumph when combined with smart work.

Some light and humorous incidents kept us energised to deal with the heavy working hours. Our dress code was business formals throughout the week and smart casuals for Fridays or if we had to work on a weekend. One good Friday morning, I entered the office dressed up as usual. Formal pants, a shirt, and my Oxford shoes. Suddenly I realised there was something strange with everybody. Everybody looked a little different. Only until I realised, "Fish, it's a Friday and I am in my formals, not the smart casuals." Since Priyanka and I lived in opposite rooms in the same Oyo, we usually had breakfast together and came to the office. This was one of the few days when that also didn't happen because our schedules were haywire. Otherwise, I would have realised my mistake at breakfast itself. Plus, when you leave work late at night and have to reach the office early the next morning, who remembers the day of the week anyway? But Oh Boy, did I allow the interns to pull my leg! Manav was putting pictures with me in all the WhatsApp groups possible, captioned "Me with my Manager". The interns were laughing every moment I passed by. I had never waited for the day to get over like I did that day.

To add to the adventure, there was a poker club called Kings and Queens just 2 km from my office. Investment banking has some of the most hectic working hours. But

I managed to take time out for poker. Be it weekends or some rare weekdays with a lesser workload, I was at the poker tables. I was sacrificing my sleep for sure but poker made my internship all the more adventurous. Poker was my way of rejuvenation.

When I look back, I realise I have infinite memories of the 2-month internship. There were times when I just felt like giving up because of the workload, but perseverance and hunger to keep learning helped me see things through. Also, my mother's favourite dialogue, "If you can survive and win under these circumstances, nothing in life will ever have the strength to pull you back", kept echoing in my ears.

I will go ahead and summarize the internship with a short email of gratitude to my team, which I wrote on the last day of my internship. Please excuse the investment banking jargon:

Dear ANZ Team,

I feel blessed to have been a part of ANZ for the past 8 weeks. Choosing ANZ has been one of the most fruitful decisions in my life to date. Starting with the work, the sector-agnostic reason for joining ANZ materialised pretty well as I got exposure to Consumer Retail, Healthcare, FIG, TMT, and a little bit of LBO (thanks to Leah), in just a short span of 2 months. I can never thank you guys enough for what you have been to me. You gave me a typical family environment away from college and home. You have acted as my mentors, and my friends and also counselled me, all at the same time. I will always cherish the memories of amazing interactions shared with all of you. Ishu's charm and simplicity and the resulting fan following, Leah's crisp and effective communication skills, Akhilesh's efforts to make sure I would learn something new with every task, Aparna's multitasking efficiency and Amrita's "What's up?" that had the same sweetness and energy at any hour of the day... I indeed have a lot to take away. I don't know what the future holds for me, whether I get to come back here, whether you guys are still here when I come back, whether I get lucky enough to join ANZ again, too many ifs, but these externalities don't matter to me. Nobody can take away from me the time I have spent here with you. I will always feel proud and happy about being associated with this team even if it was for a short period. Will surely want to keep in touch with everyone.

Believe it or not, extending your gratitude to people who have helped you in your journey to becoming better is one of the most beautiful ways to keep yourself happy and positive.

Ambition and its Costs

After enjoying the three-day break between the internship and Term IV in Bangalore, which was full of catching up with old friends and Poker, I was back on campus. The storm of the internship had ended and there was silence, all over again. It was so good to be back. The campus was no less than a home and the working hours during the internship made the PGDM course seem like a vacation. The number of courses also gets reduced in the second year. We had ample time to rejoice with friends and share our internship experiences. There was a lot of time to talk to our families. Papa's preventive chemotherapy was over now and after the tests, doctors had declared him free of cancer. No more chemotherapy. He just had to go for a follow-up check-up in September. It was a huge sigh of relief for the entire family. Papa even started spending a few hours in the office every day.

He had started regaining his health and his target was to become perfectly fit before my convocation on 7th April 2018. Life was beautiful again.

Soon, PPO results started coming in. It was another reality check for me. Most students who did not get a PPO were heartbroken and visibly demoralized. Others whose results were still not out were tensed to the core. I was still in relaxation mode and deep down I had a strong feeling that I would get my PPO from Silverlight. My review meetings had been excellent, even better than I could have hoped for. More than anything else, I was satisfied with the kind of effort I had put into the internship, both physically and mentally. If I had still not gotten a PPO, it would have been because of externalities beyond my control. This relaxed mindset made me a little complacent, to be honest. People with PPO rejections, although demotivated initially, had started working hard.

One thing about my B-School life that I strongly regret is not having seriously participated in any case competition. These case competitions are organised by the top MNCs and are focused on solving real-world problems, to which students present innovative and practical solutions. Winners get a job offer or a direct interview with these companies. So, I had comfortably assumed that I needn't work hard for it because I already had a dream job offer (because of the expected PPO). But then I saw my peers working day and night for these competitions, winning them, meeting the CEOs of these corporations, confidently pitching ideas in their board rooms, traveling to different cities and in some rare cases, other countries. They were implementing their MBA skills in the real world in the best ways possible. And I had instant regrets. It was too late until I realised what I had missed out on. Opportunities kept knocking on my door but my complacency didn't let me open the door. During the internship, I never got complacent because of the clear goal of PPO in mind. But here, I failed to realise how the case competitions could have helped me grow and complacency won. I don't even know if I was good enough to win those competitions, but what I do regret is that I did not make the effort.

My strong advice to anybody who attends B-School, irrespective of whether you get a PPO or not, is don't let go of working hard for these case competitions. I genuinely feel that the first-hand exposure that comes along with both success and failure in these competitions is one of the most important learnings from your B-School. You are competing with the best of the best, literally. Learn from my mistakes, rather than learning after committing the same mistakes yourselves, be the smarter person.

The time just after the internship pushed me into a deep pensive mode. There comes a time, at least once, in everybody's life, when they start questioning the meaning of life. The entire two months of my internship were only about the internship. No family, no friends. Just office colleagues and office friends. I was fulfilling my ambition, but it had its costs. It made my decision to be an entrepreneur in the long run even more concrete. Not because being an entrepreneur would involve fewer working hours, but because I could have gained the freedom to be accountable for my own time. I had always wanted to do business with Papa and learn from him. It was my dream to become capable enough to work alongside him. I did want to join Silverlight after my MBA but for a limited time. I wanted to gain the best of exposure and convert that into becoming a successful entrepreneur under Papa's guidance.

Not being with Papa during his most trying times is the biggest cost of ambition that I have ever had to pay. So, the next aim was to fulfill the ambition of being an IIM grad and set further ambitions only after calculating the costs. I had to make sure that I did not fall into the rosy trap of the corporate world and focus on accomplishing what I had originally wanted, which was, "Staying close to the roots". I still wanted to travel in a chauffeur-driven car, sit in the back seat, and while looking out through the window, dream of owning a part of this beautiful world. But I wanted to do it on my terms. I wanted to make sure that like my father and uncles, I put family above everything else. The satisfaction they derive while going all-in for the family is a treat for the eyes and strongly inspires me to become a better person.

Another contribution to this thought process was the course LIDA (Leadership: Inspiration, Dilemmas, and Action) by Prof. Unnikrishnan, one of the most respected professors in the institute. He had done enormous research to introduce this course to us. The course involved reading some critically acclaimed books that made us question the meaning of life in one form or the other and making presentations about them in class.

One such book was *Siddhartha* by Hermann Hesse. I had some life-transforming takeaways from the book. It stresses the importance of having clarity in your goals, letting go when the chosen path or decision no longer seems correct, and being able to make use of disguised opportunities in your favour.

In one instance, Govinda tells Siddhartha that if Siddhartha had stayed with the Samanas (monks), he would have soon learned to walk on water. Siddhartha's reply to this was one that has gotten etched in my memory, "I do not seek to walk on water. Let old Samanas be content with such feats." This statement made me question the entire ecosystem operating around us.

Most of us end up becoming a part of the race that we never chose for ourselves. Be it FOMO (fear of missing out), herd mentality, or fear of taking the road less travelled, we find ourselves in a place that we had not wanted to land in. On top of that, some of us managed to win that race also. But once the race is won, even before the joy of winning fades away, we question ourselves, now what? Some of the sensible ones manage to contain the joy for longer times and reward themselves for the hard work they put in. But the over-ambitious ones just end up becoming prisoners of their ambition, which keeps pushing them to set the next big goal. Unfortunately, I was one of them. I had not been like that always. However once I started growing professionally, I became addicted to the kick that one receives from success. The kick becomes the driving force. Fix a goal, work your ass off towards it, achieve it, and pleasure your senses with the kick it gives you. But with time, this becomes so monotonous that the kick gets lost somewhere in the middle. You just end up becoming a machine in the factory of life, that sets a goal, toils endlessly, achieves the goal, and moves on to set the next goal. No time to chew the cud. No more respect for the kick.

Sometimes just questioning the authenticity of things surrounding you gives you answers to the other questions you never knew existed in the first place. The question "Why MBA?" had at least 50 (on the conservative side) different answers during the IIM interviews for the 384 people in the batch. By now, the answers had reduced to just 5, "I want to join BCG", "I want to join Silverlight", "I want to join HUL", "I want to join ITC", and "I want to join Microsoft." Very few of us now had answers on lines different from the above. I was also a victim of this to some extent. I started doing some research on what IIM grads do over their lifetimes after graduation. I found out some startling facts. A lot of studies claim that a millennial is expected to go through 10-15 job changes over his lifetime and around 8 career changes. This was primarily because of the ever-changing technological infrastructure and the corresponding skill-set requirement, along with the changing preferences of millennials. What I realised is that the time you get in a B-School is perfect to help you explore different career options for your future and prepare yourselves for them. This was a crucial learning from my IIM experience.

Few students in the batch were seriously preparing for UPSC along with an MBA. It was inspiring to observe them. I had always wanted to become a writer. I had known that most good writers were voracious readers and I had never been much of a reader. I used the remaining time to read books and eventually turned it into a habit. I also started attending some online story-telling workshops. It's just the thought process that counts, it does not involve a lot of extra effort as one would imagine. For the MBA aspirants reading this, I strongly urge you to try preparing yourselves for alternative career options, while you are at your dream B-Schools. You would want a stable job to start with to repay your educational loan. But that will be repaid in a few years, what after that? In this fast-changing and competitive world, it doesn't harm you to develop an alternative skill. First, it highly boosts your confidence whenever you learn something new. Second, the more career options you build for yourself, the lesser the costs you will have to bear to fulfill your ambitions.

Talking about the costs of ambition would be incomplete without mentioning the coolest professor at my IIM, Prof. Pankaj Baag. He took the course Commercial Bank Management in Term IV. He had done his FPM from IIM Calcutta at the age of forty and lived life on his terms. We never saw him getting mad at anybody, no matter what. He just knew how to maintain his composure and deal with any situation with utter calmness. He was one of those professors who never believed in exerting authority to prove a point. His talks were the sweetest of all, he spoke with such innocence and genuineness. His classes were always full of fun and light humour. And there was some subtlety in his humour, which kept cautioning us from crossing the line between being ambitious and over-ambitious. Now that I look back, I realise that I had some really good professors who made a difference in so many lives.

The next phase of the IIM journey was the ultimate dream for a lot of us, the Foreign Exchange Program. Students who opt for this program pursue Term V at one of the foreign universities that the institute has tie-ups with, most of them being in Europe. I had been excited about this program right from the day I joined the institute. Even more excited was Papa, for me to go on this program. There is hardly anything else that can match the exposure gained through studying in a foreign university and exploring different parts of the world while traveling at the same time. What followed were the three most eventful months of my life.

Seventh Heaven

The foreign exchange program is a one-of-a-kind experience. You are left free to explore a new continent for a good three months, improve your money management skills, enhance your planning efficiency, meet new people, try an infinite number of food cuisines (although not as great for vegetarians like me), improve your communication skills, broaden your mindsets by observing different cultures and get exposure to the European education system, all at the same time. Not to forget, the foreign exchange program takes place at a time when you are at the most energetic phase of your life and you also have lesser responsibilities. No matter how much money you have at forty, it's highly unlikely that you will have the time to travel around like a free bird for three months without any hard-hitting responsibilities. My strong suggestion to all MBA aspirants is don't let go of this opportunity. Banks are there to fund your exchange programs at minimum rates of interest. You can earn the money later but you can't get this opportunity later. It will change your outlook toward life for the better.

Three months of the exchange program finally felt like an actual reward for all the hard work we had been putting in throughout the years leading up to this. When we are in the 10th standard, we are told that we should do well in board exams and then life would be fun. Even before the 10th standard results are out, we join coaching institutes and start preparing for competitive exams combined with 12th standard board exams. We work tirelessly for two years to ace the entrance exams. But the moment we enter college, we start focusing on CAT/GATE/GRE/GMAT or start preparing to land a plush job for ourselves. The struggle and hard work just keep continuing. But with the foreign exchange program, it felt like the donkey finally got its carrot.

Those are the three months in Europe, where you reap the benefits of your decade-long labour. You are a free bird and can plan your three months exactly the way you want. Planning ensures that you don't regret missing out on things that you would have otherwise wanted to experience. Every day in the program makes you feel like you couldn't have asked for more.

Lille, France was my base in Europe, where my foreign university was located. Mohit, Vikas, Neeraj, Dhruvi, and Anjana, my friends from the campus, were going to be my family for the next three months. 28th August 2017, the Delhi International Airport was bustling with students from top B-Schools across India who were ready to embark on their foreign exchange journeys in Europe. The ripples of our enthusiasm and excitement seemed to circle the entire airport.

After a tiring flight to Paris and then the onward train from Paris to Lille, we finally reached our Airbnb. We quickly dumped our luggage at the apartment in a haphazard manner and left for a refreshing stroll on the streets of Lille. Lille is a typical student city with its vibrant youth and happening streets. Soon, we stopped at an open bar, right in the city centre and helped ourselves to some local varieties of chilled beer. It was such a pleasant evening, perfect weather, cool breeze, and booze, with the best of company. That evening, we were just dreaming about the places we would visit in the coming three months, the new experiences we would have, and the memories we would take back with us for the rest of our lives. It all appeared to be a fairy tale and we had just entered the fairyland.

After spending a beautiful evening, we returned to our Airbnb. I had not taken a sim card yet so had no internet while I was out. The moment I connected to the Wi-Fi, I could see multiple messages on WhatsApp. When I had just thought that the day couldn't have gotten any better, the first news that came to me from India was that I had been offered a PPO from Silverlight.

Just what my eyes had been longing to read. I was on cloud nine. Days and nights of hard work during The internship had finally paid off. Like the internship offer, Vikas was the first person I told about the PPO. The biggest reason for my happiness was that a PPO from one of the top Investment Banks in the world got me closer to becoming a more capable and independent individual in the eyes of Papa. Thinking of how proud Papa would be, I had tears in my eyes. I don't think anything else has ever mattered more to me. Proving Papa right about his expectations of me is always the most satisfying feeling as a son. It was way past midnight in India, but I couldn't control the child in me, I immediately called Maa Papa. The frequency of my voice was nowhere close to normal, I was simply ecstatic. On hearing the news, they were elated, happy, proud and like the perfect father, Papa said, "This is just the beginning for you my son, the sky's the limit." Maa replied, "I had known it all along Beta, you had to get the PPO." The conviction with which mothers make these claims makes it impossible to contest (even though sometimes the claims are implausible). We talked for a while reminiscing about the hard times during the internship and how not giving up made all the difference in the end. It was the seventh heaven for me. I was at the highest peak in my life, the orgasm of life if I may say so. I had a PPO from Silverlight, Papa no longer had cancer and was regaining his health, the family business was doing good, I was about to be a graduate from one of the top B-Schools in the country and I was going to travel across Europe for the next three months with all the above positive things in the back of my head. Pure bliss!

I was prepared to make the best use of my time in Europe. Living at an Airbnb in Europe was a different experience altogether. In India, we have the luxury and privilege of hiring domestic help for daily household chores. At Lille, there was no such thing. The six of us had divided tasks amongst ourselves. We used to cook one meal a day and have one meal outside. Two meals and some snacks could get us through the day easily. We had begun to realise the value of the hostel mess back at the IIM campus from day one itself. Cleaning the floor, taking the trash out, and doing the dishes, we were totally on our own and the six of us lived like a family for three months. While travelling, Subway was the saviour for vegetarians like me. Healthy, hygienic, and comparatively cheaper offerings made it the preferred choice for us. We also had students from different nationalities staying close by. Pooling our resources to organise poker nights and relaxation parties on weekends is one of my most cherished memories of living in Europe.

One fine afternoon, I was walking towards a sim card store after college but lost my way in the middle. A charming brunette with twinkling green eyes was passing by and I asked her if she knew about the place. Fortunately, she knew English. She knew where the store was and since she was going in the same direction, she offered to walk with me to the SIM card store. Her name was Nicole. She was from Bolivia and was also an exchange student at my institute. She had been living in Lille for over a year now. She showed me to the store and we ended up making plans to meet again in the evening. And from that evening, started a beautiful bond of friendship where we walked through the streets of Lille for hours together every other day. She had this beautiful quality of getting the listener excited about her shenanigans. Be it talking about her family or life in Bolivia, the cultures in South America, or her experiences in France, she was full of enthusiasm. It was delightful to have met Nicole. It's mind-boggling to understand the mindsets and upbringings of people from different nationalities.

At the institute, we were supposed to have 1 course per week and we were supposed to do 8 courses for our minimum requirement of 12 Indian credits. The six of us had chosen subjects and the weeks in a way that we had some empty weeks in between to ourselves, to explore the other parts of Europe. Although life at Lille was very different, it merely took us a week to get comfortable with it. We walked for almost 5 km daily and it soon became a habit. Lille and Europe in general, opened my senses to the pleasure one could derive from walking. The essence of any city is best felt by walking through it, absorbing every wave of energy the different parts of the city carry along with them. I started being more observant of the finer details of how people lived as I walked in step with them. More than anything else, walking kept me fit by compensating for all the junk food I ended up munching while I was travelling during the course breaks.

In Time

As students, what's inevitable are the last-moment assignment submissions that offer an adrenaline rush like no other. There was a course called "CRM (Customer Relationship Management) in Small Business" at the institute and I had a fellow exchange student Rahul Verma from IIM Bangalore in this course. It was the last day of the course and I received a text from Rahul in the morning asking me to get my laptop to college. He wanted to do some work on it and had packed his laptop for a trip, so couldn't bring his own. I had already left for the college without my laptop when I saw his message. The class began at 8:15 am. I saw Rahul desperately trying to arrange for a laptop. Finally, he managed to borrow a laptop from another classmate and quickly started writing answers to some questions. On questioning him as to what he was trying to achieve came his reply, "Dude, don't you remember that we have to submit an assignment for this course before 9 am? Did you think I was struggling for a laptop to watch porn at 8 in the morning?" Damn! I had thought the deadline was 9 pm. I quickly arranged for another laptop and started finishing my pending assignment, I had already completed 70% of it beforehand. To complete the rest, I frantically collated relevant information and added my analysis with a sharply focused mind. Did I manage to submit it in time? Well, let's just say that the last-minute submission was quite literal that day. I uploaded the assignment at 8:59 am. JUST IN TIME!

During the foreign exchange program, we were hopping countries like it was going from one block to another at the IIM campus. Every other week, we were in a different European country, being introduced to a different culture, a different language, a different lifestyle, and a different vibe.

There was so much to explore and so little time. This meant planning journeys with train transfers of less than five minutes quite frequently. The enthusiasm to de-board one train, search for the platform number for the next, reach that platform, and board another one, all in a total of fewer than five minutes, was the kind of adrenaline rush we were almost addicted to. You enter the train with the door closing right behind you and you give a high-five to your friend while breathing heavily because of the run and simultaneously laughing your hearts out because you made it, JUST IN TIME!

During one of the breaks, we were attending Oktoberfest in Germany which is the largest beer festival in the world. I had planned the trip in such a way that I would have attended the festival from morning to noon and taken the 2:30 pm train back to Lille (on a Saturday). I had a flight from Paris (an hour from Lille) to Iceland on Sunday.

We reached our Oktoberfest tent at around 10 in the morning. It was huge, with hundreds of people dancing and singing along to the tunes of cultural German songs. It was the most joyous setting. And, the beer glasses were delightfully large, each glass holding 1 litre of beer alone. It was the perfect heaven for anybody who wanted to leave all their worries behind and live in the moment, the happy high was infectious. In a jiffy, it was 2 pm and it was time for my "Au Revoir". But my friends just weren't ready to let me go. "Sid, we are all having such a great time, we don't know when we will get such a time together again, you just can't go." I politely said, "But guys, I have already bought the train tickets. Moreover, the next train to Lille is at night, I have to catch tomorrow's flight for Iceland anyhow."

No listening, they made me tear my tickets and I did not board that train. That entire day's experience was priceless and rejuvenating for the mind.

We finally left the tent around 5 in the evening and my next train to Lille was at 10 pm. That too wasn't a direct train and I had to make around 10 transfers during the entire journey from Munich to Lille, all during the night. Dead tired after a sleepless night full of train and bus transfers and waiting at deserted stations, I reached Lille at 11:30 am on Sunday. My friends were waiting for me, we had to shift our luggage from one apartment to another before going to Iceland because we had a different Airbnb booked for the rest of the stay. It was a one-hour bus journey from Lille to Paris airport and the flight was at 4 pm. We packed our luggage, cleaned the apartment, shifted the luggage to the other apartment, and somehow managed to catch the 1 pm bus to Paris. Phew! Reached the Paris airport at 2 pm, but Knock Knock! We had to wait another half an hour inside the bus at the Paris airport because some checking for terror suspects was going on. The entire bus was checked and nobody was allowed to get down. Murphy's law indeed! Finally, at 3:00 pm, we ran towards the check-in counter and made the boarding, JUST IN TIME. I couldn't feel my senses, my body was completely exhausted after Oktoberfest and the never-ending travel saga. I slept like a baby on the flight.

I have been to a total of twenty countries as I am writing this and Iceland is THE most beautiful and picturesque country of all. We went on a road trip across southern Iceland, where the landscape/skyline used to change every thirty minutes along the drive. From waterfalls to raw mountains, from glaciers to lagoons, from beaches to lush green grasslands, Iceland had so much to offer. We went snorkelling at Silfra, which is a fissure created by the North American and

Eurasian tectonic plates. The water was freezing at 2 degrees Celsius and our bodies were numb even after being under thermal snorkelling suits. Then there was The Blue Lagoon, a geothermal natural spa which is literally how one usually picturises heaven in his mind. The water body with natural minerals and a soothing temperature, strong waterfalls that give you a body massage, and mist floating in the air, bliss indeed. I just wished for time to stand still.

Namaste Budapest

The foreign exchange program was a life-changing experience for so many people. For instance, Stuti, my bench partner during classes and a great friend, was a girl from Delhi, who had never stepped out of Delhi before her MBA. And there she was, travelling all across Europe, interacting and bonding with people she had never met before, exploring a different world altogether.

One morning in Budapest, Stuti and I went on a guided walking tour organised by our hostel. While we were walking, there was a group of 5-6 American guys and girls along with us who were constantly complaining about how their parents kept pestering them and didn't just let them be. Suddenly, one guy commented, "My mother keeps saying, that people from India are starving and you on the other hand have no respect for food at all." He said that in a demeaning tone implying that he was way superior to Indians just because he was an American and that it was not his job to bother about people starving in some random nation. What he didn't realise was that two Indians were walking along with him in the group. Or maybe he just did not care.

My instinct reminded me of Akshay Kumar's speech from the movie Namaste London, but neither did I have a script nor was I, Akshay Kumar. This was a real-life situation and I didn't want to make a fool of myself by giving him a lecture about India. So I came up with a plan.

We were about to purchase some refreshments to compliment the stunning city view at the end of the walking tour. I went up to the tour guide and asked him to announce that it was my birthday (made it up) and everything the group bought from the supermarket was on me. People were elated and helped themselves with chilled beers, croissants, sodas, chocolates, and other munchies. Everybody started thanking me for the beers and wished me a happy birthday. We (Stuti and I) started bonding with the Americans and had a good time with them after reaching the viewpoint. It's so natural to gel and bond when you leave all prejudices behind. As my friend Mohit Parikh (author of Manan) likes to say, "There will be no issues in the world if people are willing to let go of their egos."

While bidding our farewells after a warm evening, the guy who had those prejudiced opinions about India said to me: "It was so nice to meet you brother, had a great time." I replied, "Same here, Mark! But I hope the next time someone says India, you remember this beer and the splendid memories of the time we have just spent together, not an inferior nation of starving children." He was embarrassed to the core. My intention was not to make him feel ashamed of himself, it was his upbringing that had built this image of India in his mind in the first place. So, I just looked at him with a smile, gave him a brotherly hug, and made promises to meet again in the future. What did it cost me? A mere 25€ (yes, beer is cheap in Europe) and a little effort. It was more than worth it because what it gave me in return was priceless.

After the walking tour, we returned to the hostel and took some rest. Budapest is one city where the Indian Rupee was stronger, 1 ₹ was around 4 Hungarian Forint at that time. This meant being able to play poker with a higher budget and I obviously couldn't let go of that opportunity. There were multiple casinos within 200 metres of my hostel. The sad part, none of them had Texas Hold'em Poker. They had Caribbean Poker where you play against the dealer. The casino managers kept telling me that no place in Budapest offered Texas Hold'em Poker. But I wasn't convinced. I looked up extensively on the internet and finally found that in a mall called Duna Plaza, there was a poker club. I reached the place but found no directions or pictures pointing me towards the poker room. It was late into the night and the other shops in the mall were already closed. I remembered a guy's comment on one of the online forums that it was on the second floor. Finally, after covering the entire perimeter of the floor, I found a separate poker cum gaming zone in one corner of the second floor. Bang! I had managed to find a Texas Hold'em Poker club in Budapest after all the casinos had told me there was none. It was an elite poker club where most of the players were locals. No wonder, as it was next to impossible for an outsider to find a poker room that is located away from the city centre, at one of the corners of the second floor, inside a mall. Passion does take you places!

Let me reveal a big secret to all of you, my beloved readers. The foreign exchange program was also a poker tour for me. Out of all the countries and cities I visited, I played poker in the casinos at each one of them. There were so many thrilling and memorable incidents on the poker tables that I could write a separate book entirely on my poker journey. In hindsight, playing poker across Europe at the best places with people from different nationalities still appears like a dream more than a reality. It's priceless. Now, the secret—my winnings from poker were just enough to cover my entire Europe trip for three months.

I will go ahead and narrate my favourite poker hand. I was playing at Casino Estoril in Portugal (this is where one of the earlier James Bond movies—*On Her Majesty's Secret Service* was shot). Blinds 1/2€, Buyin—100€. I was dealt 6-7 suited at middle position and called a raise of

12€ pre-flop. I had been playing very tight (no bluffing) for almost 3 hours now and this was the time to take advantage of my image. I bluffed a guy who folded an Ace pair because I could make him believe that I had a set of sixes. I won the 250€ pot and my opponent (also the best player on the table) commented, "I am sure you have two 6s in your hand." I wickedly showed him my hand (6-7) and replied, "Sir, you are partially correct." People at the table went crazy, "Where are you from young man?", "Oh India is great", and "Welcome to Estoril", were the phrases I was greeted with. I played for 10 more minutes and before I could give any chance to the guy I had bluffed to recover his money, I politely got up, wished the players well, and left the casino with a stuffed wallet.

Yesterday's Gone

As they say, bad times don't last forever. But so do good times. I was having the time of my life but fate had other plans. In hindsight, it's easier to convince yourself with this fate crap and accept whatever happened. But the exact moment when something life-changing happens within a blink of an eye challenges the entire existence of the person. You can't even figure out what hit you in the first place, digesting the consequences of the hit is still secondary.

Sometime during the second week of November, I was in Brussels, Belgium for a weekend trip. After a regular poker session at night, I was walking towards the bus station to board my return bus to Lille. I had just left the casino when I received a call from Maa. She was crying incessantly on the phone and with a trembling voice informed me that Papa's cancer had resurfaced. This time, it had metastasized to some parts of the liver and the abdominal walls. When Papa had gone for a follow-up checkup in September, there were some tests done. The reports that finally came in October confirmed the reoccurrence of cancer, but Papa didn't allow anybody to tell me about it. His chemotherapy had started again in October and he had not been responding well to it. Despite his condition, on every phone call, Papa kept telling me that he was healthy and that I should keep making the best of my foreign exchange program and explore as much as I could. He was still upset with me that I could not find time to visit the Scandinavian countries. I had no idea of his miseries whatsoever.

Papa was asleep when Maa informed me about this, and I just froze on the street. Time stopped for me and everything just stood still. I went blank. With whatever energy I could gather, I consoled Maa and told her that I would prepone my return tickets to India. My last class was on 24th November, so I could prepone my tickets from 5th December to 25th November.

I was walking on the street to the bus station, with absolutely no idea of what was going on around me. I had turned into a machine that just knew it had to walk towards the bus station. I was walking along the footpath, and suddenly I saw a man pacing towards me. I tried to ignore him, but in a flash, he had cornered me to a wall and was pointing a gun at me. Maybe he had followed me from the casino and waited until he could corner me at a spot obstructed by the cars parked on the street. I had never even seen a real gun before. He started threatening me for money and I just stood there, completely numb. My mind was completely occupied with the conversation I had had on the phone with Maa. I just could not process what was happening. I could not even understand the language he spoke. My silence, which was because of my absent-mindedness, gave him an indication that I was not afraid of him and was trying to act smart. In his obvious frustration, he punched me in the face, and I fell on the ground hitting the grill on the side. He then began threatening me in an even louder voice.

It took one more thump from him before I got back to my senses and quickly started reaching for my wallet. Just when I was about to pull out money and give it to him, a group of young guys who were walking on the street saw us and rushed to help me. The robber who got visibly scared ran away. I breathed a sigh of relief and started crying like a baby. I was bleeding from the side of my forehead and my collar was torn. Those guys helped me get up from the ground, offered me water, and brought some first aid from a nearby market. They walked with me till I safely reached the bus station. I can never thank those heaven-sent angels enough. They saved me when there was no ray of light reaching my way. That bus journey from Brussels to Lille was one of the toughest journeys I have had to date. This fall from seventh heaven brought back so many memories of past ups and downs. And this very incident was the unfortunate turn towards bad luck that stayed with me for a very long time from then on.

Back at Lille, I did not tell anybody about the "Under the Gun" incident or Papa's cancer, except for two people, Mohit and Nicole. You don't feel vulnerable after sharing anything with Mohit, he is just there for you, unconditionally. And walks with Nicole used to be the perfect stress busters. After returning from Brussels, I told her about the incidents and she was there for me, all along, just like Mohit. I was a changed person during the last leg of the exchange program. No more weekend trips, no more outings, just the regular classes and the evening walks with Nicole. I was dying to return home and be with my family. My other flatmates were completely balled up, they just could not understand what had happened to me. Whenever they made any plans for an outing, I used to invariably take a rain check and opt-out. I was no longer the same SidJ. It's quite an uncomfortable mental zone to be in. People notice a change in your behaviour, they ask you questions that you are not ready to answer. But it does keep things simple. And complicating things was the last bit my mind needed at that time.

The Permanent Void

Right after I returned from Europe on 26th November 2017, we had to immediately take Papa to Medanta, Delhi again as his health was deteriorating day by day. Somewhere in the second week of December, while I was still in the hospital, I received my grade for the last course during the exchange program called "Managing Teams". I failed with a score of 9.6/20, where 10/20 was the passing score. I had never failed in my entire academic life, even in a trivial unit test. This was a brutal punch in the face. Now, I thought there was some mistake in the grading because who fails in a course that did not even have an exam, only assignments? Not even in my distant dreams did I anticipate the storm those 0.4 marks were about to set off. I kept my calm and sent an email to my Professor, to recheck if she had received all my assignment submissions. I got an automated reply saying that she would be out of the office till 2nd January, of course, Christmas and New Year holidays in Europe. And this is when Murphy's Law started defining my life.

Even after spending around two weeks in the Hospital, Papa's health did not improve. On 15th December, after his routine visit, Dr Randhir Sud called me and my Uncle outside the room to discuss Papa's condition. He said, "Sadly, there is nothing left that we can do, Mr. Praduman only has a few days left now, I suggest you take him home." Chachu gathered some courage while being thoroughly shaken and said, "Sir, okay, we will take him home, but in case a miracle happens and his condition starts showing any signs of improvement, we will bring him back to you." Dr. Sud's reply still echoes in my ears, "Mr. Jain, the problem with miracles is that they only happen to others, you only hear about them, never experience them." Chachu and I were completely broken, with absolutely no words. Both of us stood silently outside the room for a good 10 minutes, without facing each other, trying to digest what the doctor had just said while holding our tears back. His words were practical, but how can you accept the fact that your father will be no more with you in a few days and that there is nothing that anybody could do about it?

I lost my Papa on 22nd December 2017. I had still not come to terms with the fact that Papa was diagnosed with cancer, losing him crushed me. Everything was so quick. Couldn't I just delete 2017 from my life? I was at the lowest point ever. He was my backbone. I could not imagine making life decisions without his guidance and approval. It was like losing the protective roof above my head. I was still blessed with a beautiful family that was there to support me at every step, but nobody can replace a father.

On the morning of the cremation, my younger sister Kanishka came up to me and said "Bhai, I also want to go to the cremation ground with you, it's not fair that I am asked to stay back just because women don't go there. He was my father as much as yours."

I said, "I promise you that I will take you with me, just hold my hand and tag along."

So many people stopped her from going. I argued with all of them and kept my promise. I had lost my father; I was least bothered about the judgements from distant relatives and society. My sister's wish was the only thing that mattered at that point. The sad part is that our society makes women plead for things that should already belong to them. He was her father, why should she be put in a situation where she has to request other people to allow her to be with him? I took her to the cremation place and made sure that we gave "Agni" to our father together. I am narrating the above incident here because I feel the courage that I mustered to take a stand for my sister originated from my education at the IIM. Professors like Anupam Das Sir and Mathew Sir have always taught us to be bold enough to take a stand against the baseless rituals our society operates on.

They emphasised that most of the religious customs and societal rituals are nothing more than ways to promote patriarchy. Our mainstream education system rarely tries to inculcate such teachings within us. Ironically, these are the teachings that help you grow in the most profound ways and in fact, should be taught starting at the primary level of education.

I hardly got any time to mourn my father's death, as my Term VI had already begun and I had to return to college. Now, I had lost all enthusiasm for my MBA, as it was Papa's dream, more than mine. During his treatment, he kept requesting the doctors to cure him before 7th April 2018 as he wanted to attend my convocation with me. He wanted to sit in my classroom and get his picture clicked with my name tag on the front as we have in IIM classrooms. Alas! None of us could fulfil his wish.

Back in college, there were times when I used to cry for hours together, alone in my room. I did not want to express my sorrows in front of my friends as I did not want to create an atmosphere of melancholy whenever I was around. Although the inner sadness and despair were killing me, I hated it when people looked at me with sympathetic eyes. I made sure that I kept myself occupied in some activity or the other. I felt that was the only way to move on.

A Tryst with Reality

Remember the course I failed? The professor finally replied in the first week of January 2018 and told me that she had failed me because I had not contributed to a group assignment. Now, this group assignment was supposed to be done in the week after the course ended, 25th November - 2nd December. I had returned to India and was in the hospital with Papa. I informed my teammates (all from different nationalities) about my situation and they assured me that they would take care of the group report and encouraged me to look after my father. However, the teacher told me that my group members had written in the peer review that I did not contribute. The partner foreign institute did not even let me take a retest (which involved the submission of an easy assignment) to pass. They said that the group assignment was a replacement for the final exam (which was not told to us before) and without contributing to the final exam, one was not allowed a retest. I explained the unfortunate situation I was in because of which I could not contribute to the group assignment, but they paid no heed to it. They said, "We can give you sympathy, but nothing more." I asked them if I could come back and redo the course altogether along with paying the fees again, but even that request was turned down.

How the system worked is that on passing every course (irrespective of marks scored), we were given 1.6 credits. We had a total of 8 courses that could have given us 12.8 credits (needed 12 minimum credits to clear Term V). On failing one course, I received 11.2 credits in total and hence fell short of 0.8 credits in Term V because of it. That could be easily made up for, right? Wrong. We have this draconian rule at the institute which says that if a student fails to get a minimum of 12 program credits during the foreign exchange program, the Term VI registration stands cancelled and the student has to repeat both Terms V and VI with the next batch. This in turn meant that the other 11.2 credits that I had gotten in the foreign exchange program would be a waste now and my entire course at the foreign institute would reduce to a ZERO because of the 0.4 marks. No other IIM has such a rule and even at my IIM, we were the first batch facing this rule. The new rule meant that I could lose my PPO from Silverlight and my graduation would have been extended by a year. In monetary terms, I already had to repay a loan of around 25 lakhs and would have had to pay the fees for Terms V and VI again. I was totally at the mercy of the institute's authorities now, to help me graduate in the same year.

It was in the first week of February when the partner Institute closed all doors. Now, the matter was with the PGP (Post Graduate Programme) Executive Committee. The PGP chairperson, Prof. Sundar Rajan was supposed to have a meeting with the committee members to discuss my issue. I had written a strong appeal to the Committee members explaining the inevitable circumstances of my case. How was it fair that my career was about to take a hit because of 0.4 marks? That too, because I had to take care of my father who was fighting cancer.

Meanwhile, I went to some of the senior faculties in the Institute to ask their advice on how to go about this issue. One of them was Prof. Rajendra Singh. He was the Head of Administration then and was the PGP Chairperson till 2016-17. He had taught Quantitative Methods to us in Term I. He got 12 poor ratings in the anonymous feedback and his next lecture was all about "How dare you give me a poor rating? If you are brave enough, come out in the open and say it to my face. What do you think of yourselves?" I think this is enough for you to understand his personality. But I had to go to him because of his position. He listened to my entire story, paused for a second, and suddenly called Prof. Sundar Rajan on the phone. He said, "Sir, there is a student here requesting help related to a foreign exchange issue, how is he still here? Why has his Term not been terminated yet?" I was shattered and furious at the same time. I had gone to him with tears in my eyes pleading for mercy and that was his response. I gathered courage and told him calmly, "Sir, if you don't want to help, that is all right, but please don't tell others not to help." His response still gnaws at me: "Okay, I will not interfere, it is anyway not under my purview." What? If it was not under your purview, why did you call Prof. Sundar Rajan in the first place? Isn't that downright evil?

Without uttering another word, I started leaving his office, dejected and helpless. He then made another statement, "I was the one who initiated that rule in the first place. You people go on foreign exchange programs and travel to 20-25 countries in 3 months. You think of it as a joke?" He was totally against the foreign exchange program. Prof. Sundar Rajan had the same opinion. He said "How is it possible that in 3-4 lakhs, you people manage to travel around so many countries? A lot of faculties are totally against this program." What I don't understand is, why is it a bad thing if a student manages to travel around 20 countries in 4 lakhs? Shouldn't our teachers be proud of our money management and budgeting skills? And who can question the importance of travelling for all-round development? If you are so against the foreign exchange program, don't offer it in the first place. Making draconian rules to spoil students' careers is not the right way to release your frustration. That too, when the case is as genuine as it can get.

There were some highly supportive and rational professors too, but I can't name them. I don't want them to be in trouble for supporting me and for being by my side. That is how the Institute authorities operated. They didn't like keeping company with professors who could take a stand for their students and were bold enough to question the system. As shocking as it may sound, that was the harsh reality of one of the top educational institutes in the country.

Roller-coaster Ride

After writing the appeal to the executive committee, I went and spoke to some of the committee members personally. One of them was Prof. Pragya Naidu (Placements' Chairperson). She was shocked to hear about my case and said, "You have a PPO from Silverlight, you are my responsibility. I will do something for you."

After waiting patiently for the meeting for a few days, it turned out that the executive committee meeting never happened since most of the members were out of campus taking admission interviews. So, the meeting happened over email and was a mere formality. I got the verdict on 15th February 2018 that my Term VI had been terminated and I would have to repeat both Terms with the next batch. It's important to mention here that along with me was another batchmate Viraj, who had failed in 2 subjects and was falling short of 2.4 credits. He was given the same verdict.

After receiving the verdict, I immediately went to Pragya Naidu Ma'am and asked her what went wrong in the meeting. She said, "I supported you but there are other committee members also, my opinion alone doesn't have any weightage." While Sundar Rajan Sir said, "There was nobody who supported your case in the meeting over email. The Executive Committee can't go against what is written in the academic handbook and only the director's appeal can help you now." I don't know who, but one of them was lying. And it was frustrating as they were supposed to be our "teachers".

Prof. Sundar Rajan is a person with whom you couldn't imagine having logical conversations. And although it used to be frustrating in the beginning, I got accustomed to it soon. He used to make comments like, "If your father had passed away during the period of that course, we would have considered your case, but since he was only unwell during that time and passed away a month later, we can't do anything." On asking him how it was fair that for 0.4 marks and the resulting deficit of 0.8 credits, I was being made to repeat two whole Terms, he said, "Yes, the rule is unfair. I will take it up for discussion for the next batch, but currently, this is the rule and nothing can be done." He always had a wicked smile on his face, that contained an element of mockery and reeked of sheer sadism.

On the same day as the Executive Committee verdict, I filed an appeal to the Director (Prof. Karan Bagchi). Appealing to the director had put a stay on the initial verdict and I was allowed to continue attending the 6th Term. After the appeal, I met a lot of faculties every day, who had an idea about the case and how our administration operates. I got to know from many of them that I was suffering because there was Viraj's case involved and that the authorities were not willing to make different decisions for two people. But isn't that the definition of discretionary power in the first place? According to them, Viraj had a very weak case and he was in this situation because of his carelessness. "Since he could not be shown mercy, I had to deal with the same fate" was what they said. I was so frequently visiting the Faculty Blocks that the security guards had become my friends and used to ring me up whenever the faculty members I wanted to meet arrived.

I was also begging every day in front of the people in the Dean's and Director's offices, trying to get some information about the status of my case. The scene in the college had become a perfect replication of my miseries when my father was admitted to Medanta, Delhi. There, I was coordinating between the Oncology and Gastro departments, while here I was coordinating between the Dean's Office and the Director's Office. The head is always a busy person, so you have to go to him through an assistant. Like doctors, some or the other faculty used to be on leave. No positive news on Friday meant the matter was postponed to Monday. All these analogies made the situation even more difficult for me. I was so demotivated by the circumstances that I did not even attend my Farewell function. Earlier, I used to be so fond of dressing up, getting pictures clicked, sharing them with Papa, and enjoying myself with the best of friends. Suddenly, there was no enthusiasm, no excitement for any event.

We were called to be given the Director's Verdict on 2nd March by the PGP Office. I was standing outside the PGP Office, waiting to be called in, for about an hour and a half. This was just like how I used to stand outside the ICU to wait for news about Papa or to meet him. Just standing outside and waiting, door opening and closing, but no news for me. People going in, coming out, people smiling, people upset, but nothing for me. The wait just seemed endless. Finally, Viraj and I were called in. We were given a letter stating that the Director had not considered our appeals and that the previous decision stood as is.

Our Term VI exams were supposed to begin on 3rd March, just the day after. I was clueless about what to do. Both of us immediately went to Bagchi Sir the same evening. I questioned him why my case didn't deserve mercy. I humbly asked him, "Sir, as my director, please tell me what I should have done as a son when my immediate family needed me the most?" He didn't answer and shifted to Viraj and said, "Gehu ke sath ghun bhi pis jata hai", meaning that I was in trouble because there was Viraj's case too. After a lot of convincing that evening, he called Sundar Rajan Sir and Devrat (Dean) Sir for an impromptu meeting. We were asked to wait outside the Director's office near the reception area. To my utter surprise, I saw all my friends waiting for me. I hadn't even told them where I was. They had exams starting the next day and without caring a bit for the same, they were just there to support me. To share my happiness in case the verdict was favourable and my sorrow in case it wasn't. I was overwhelmed with mixed feelings of gratitude and shame at the same time. I felt blessed and proud of the fact that if not anything else, I had at least developed some very strong friendships during my MBA.

Soon, we were called in and the Director decided to show mercy. We were finally told that we were being allowed to write Term VI exams and that we would be given a project after the exams to make up for the deficit credits. The same verdict for both of us. Sundar Rajan Sir said, "You will get your degree with the next batch, but you will get a course completion certificate after the project so that you can join your job. The degree coming later wouldn't matter. I, myself, got my degree 4 years after graduation." Sundar Rajan Sir getting his degree 4 years later wasn't of any relevance here but I was more than happy as we no longer had to repeat Terms V and VI. Finally, a sigh of relief! My friends were elated. But I had forgotten to smile. The episodes right from my father's death to dealing with the system at my IIM and fighting for my career subconsciously made me believe that it was a sin for me to smile. Sometimes I used to catch myself smiling and immediately stop while telling myself, "You don't deserve to smile, look around you, everything is going down for you, one by one."

The first exam was on the subject Competitive strategy of Poker. Yes, we had Poker as a subject! All thanks to Deepak Dhayanithi Sir for introducing this course. The smart, lean, and bald professor used to blow people away with his witty humour, which he expressed while squinting his right eye and with a smile full of sarcasm. Also, till then, he was the only professor in India, who was teaching Poker as a course.

My friends planned to take me out to my favourite restaurant the same night. I resisted because I wanted them to study. I didn't want them to ruin their exams because of me but they insisted, "Don't forget that tomorrow's exam is Poker and that you are SidJ. We will have a good dinner and then you teach all of us for the exam tomorrow after we return, win-win." I would have taught them even if we didn't go out and they knew that. But they were just looking for ways to make me feel good. We had a good dinner and although I felt blessed to be around such friends, I just couldn't feel the happiness. Something still didn't feel right. Maybe because my gut knew that my relief was going to be short-lived. Who had imagined, this was only a way in which destiny was playing with me? There was more to come. The roller coaster had not ended just yet.

The Dance of Bureaucracy

Term VI was all about dealing with the bane of bureaucracy and learning to manage stress. I suddenly had heartfelt empathy for the character "Musaddi Lal" from the evergreen sitcom "Office Office". My joining at Silverlight was supposed to be on 16th April 2018. I had to make sure that I had completed my project formalities before that. Exams were scheduled from 3rd to 9th March. I went to Sundar Rajan Sir on 5th March, requesting him to start the project soon. He replied in an irritated tone with an apparent discomfort on his face, "Some faculty members are not in favour of the Director changing his decision. Anyway, you come after exams." As much as I had begun to understand, he was referring to Rajendra Singh because of the phone call I have mentioned about earlier.

I waited for yet another week before I could go begging for the Project again. Even after the week, he said, "The Director has not given anything in writing and I cannot start the project until that happens. I believe that you will mostly have to repeat the two Terms with the next batch, as mentioned before. In any case, you have to wait for at least 10 more days for any decision." What? Are you serious? I immediately went to the Director. He answered, "I am waiting for a proposal from the PGP, it will take some time." Now they were simply passing the ball to each other's courts and I couldn't even understand why. That is when the dance of bureaucracy began.

I went back to Sundar Rajan Sir again and told him what the Director had said. While I was talking to him, the Director called on his office phone. He had just called to tell Sundar Rajan Sir to inform us that the project was still under consideration. At that moment, I saw a different side of Sundar Rajan Sir. He almost stood up on his chair while talking to the Director, "Sir, sir, I am sorry Sir. I did not send these students to you. I had no intention of disturbing you, Sir. I am Sorry Sir. But these people are not leaving me alone, Sir. They are coming to me again and again." He either felt significantly inferior to the Director or just wanted to make sure that he remained in his good books at any cost. I was appalled that words as timid as these were coming from the mouth of the PGP Chairperson at an IIM. Didn't his position deserve a little more self-respect? I felt helpless that I had to deal with such low-esteem behaviour because my career was in his hands;

deep down, I strongly wished somebody in his position had a little more spine.

Now, the hostels were emptying. Students were either going on grad trips or going home. I was stuck in the haunting hostel, devoid of any other students. Every day of waiting was just increasing my stress and anxiety. I had started going to the gym and reading books on positivity to keep myself motivated, but nothing seemed to work after a point.

Meanwhile, the Term VI results were out and I had gotten my first A+. Of course in the subject of the Competitive Strategy of Poker. Cherry on the cake, my friend Arpita, whom I had taught the night before the exam and who was a poker noob, also got an A+. It was her first A+ as well and she was ecstatic. But my happiness was short-lived, as my mind soon got diverted to the uncertainties revolving around my life. The uncertainty of graduating with my batch and the inevitable fear of losing the hard-earned PPO from Silverlight was eating me up. My strength and support system during these times of stress was my entire family and some close friends. These angels stood by me, no matter what, and kept motivating me.

Every morning started with patiently waiting for the project to get started and ended with waiting for the next morning. On one of these days, I broke down and couldn't help missing Papa. I got myself together to pen the feelings down. "I miss you, Papa, where are you? I need you the most with me right now. In this time of crisis, I have no one to look up to. I am trying hard to stay strong, to not give up, and to keep working for that positive outcome, no matter how much time it takes, but I don't think I have it in me now, I don't have any strength left. I made you proud till your last breath, but I turned out to be a failure right after you left me. This makes me wonder if the success was ever mine. It was always you, who was holding my hand helping me make the right decisions, pushing me to grab opportunities and conquer challenges."

After innumerable visits to the PGP, Dean's, and Director's Offices and more than 10 days of paralysed waiting, I was finally called to be given the verdict by the PGP office. The promise of giving a project had vanished into thin air. Both Viraj and I were asked to repeat Term V with the next batch and in the institute's language, we were shown mercy by waiving off the repetition of Term VI. Again, the same verdict for both of me and Viraj. I immediately went to the Director to question the verdict. The only thing he could manage to say was, "We can't look at two cases differently and my hands are tied. Sorry, I cannot help you. This is the maximum mercy I can show to you." I tried to reason with the Director a lot, but he paid no heed to any argument and said that had the executive committee given a recommendation in my favour, he could have helped me. On the other hand, the members of the executive committee said that they couldn't recommend anything against the rulebook, only the Director had the power to do so. And the blame game continued. Such a timid system, with no human being courageous enough to take a stand. The toughest thing for me was to accept the rationality that I was being given that punishment just because there was another weak case involved. I was given no other justification for a verdict as harsh as this. It was too hard to digest, that too after dealing with a level of stress and anxiety I didn't even know existed before.

Keep Fighting or Get Knocked Out

Punch-Drunk! There was hardly any time for me to get up before I received the next punch. I had started experiencing anxiety attacks. I had never faced anything like it before, even remotely. The mental trauma was worse than any physical pain I had ever experienced. Suddenly, you lose all confidence in yourself and start feeling worthless. Most of the books on positivity only make sense when you are already in a positive frame of mind. It is very hard for a depressed person to come out of depression just by reading books on positivity.

You tend to shut down any advice from the outside world. On multiple occasions, I contemplated leaving everything behind and moving to a completely different place, starting afresh, probably in another country, where nobody knew me.

I was on antidepressants by now. Only my family doctor who had prescribed them to me knew about it. I could not trouble my family members more by letting them know of the anxiety attacks I was dealing with. After dealing with this for a few days, rather than being a victim of circumstances, I decided to stand my ground, come what may.

I switched from defence to offence mode and was ready to go all in. Parting words from the Director to me at the end of the final verdict meeting were, "Siddharth, I am amazed by the kind of composure you have shown in the last two months. Even after such circumstances in your family, you did not lose character and I admire you even more than before now. I don't even want to compare you with others in terms of how bravely and respectfully you have dealt with us. Mark my words, this strength of character and composure will take you a long way. This is a small incident in your life, don't get depressed by it." I humbly replied, "Sir, I am not weak. I am confident that ten years down the line, I will become a highly successful person. But sadly, I can't pay my current bank loan just with strength and positivity. Anyway, thank you for your time."

The very next day, I went to meet the Dean, Devrat Sir, probably just for closure. Let me narrate the entire meeting with him.

"Sir, on 2nd March, I was promised a project. I don't have it in writing, but there were 6 people in the room when that happened, including you. How can you go back on your word?"

"You put the Director under too much pressure. Why did you go to him late in the evening that day?"

"Sir, I had exams starting the next day and I was told that my Term VI was terminated. How could I not go to the Director the same evening?" (I was seriously astounded when he said that I had put the Director under too much pressure. I had my final exams starting the very next morning and I had no idea whether I would be allowed to write them or not but apparently, it was the Director who was under pressure. Epic indeed!)

"Anyway, we allowed you to write the exams, but the project was still under consideration."

"Sir, then on 2nd March, you should have told me that you would give the final verdict after the exams if it was still under consideration. How can you promise me, make me wait for the project for almost 20 days, and then go back on your word?"

"Okay, it was a mistake. Now, what?"

"Okay, Sir." (I was furious and speechless at the same time. Although I love my IIM dearly, I was ashamed to be dealing with such an administration. You can't just say that it was a mistake and get away with it. Had they never heard of the word accountability?)

"What we can do for you is talk to Silverlight about your case."

"No Sir, I don't want the Institute or you to vouch for me in front of Silverlight. They have seen me work for

2 months. If they think I am deserving, they can let the offer stay, else, they can revoke the offer. I don't mind. I don't want any help from the institute."

He was visibly taken aback, maybe because I had stopped begging.

Immediately after that, I called the head of the Investment Banking Division at Silverlight, Bangalore, and told him about the entire case. He was furious with the institute and promised me that my offer would not be revoked. He just instructed the HR team to get in touch with me to document the facts of the case. This meant that I could complete my 5th Term from September - December 2018 and then join Silverlight. Finally, I got some motivation to keep believing in myself.

But, I wasn't willing to accept the verdict so easily, after all this harassment by the Institute. I knew I wasn't ready to become a scapegoat or let the authorities make an example out of punishing me, just because they were against the foreign exchange program. Believe me, the kind of people I dealt with and the system they have in place, have the ultimate power to drive any normal human insane. I mean it literally, INSANE. You could lose all your senses while dealing with them.

I decided to take the matter to court. But now, the promise of a project and the fact that I was not shown mercy because there was another case involved, were useless arguments. Since they were not in writing, they would not stand in court (verbal agreements are not considered to be strong enough in reality). Other than pleading for mercy from the court because of my circumstances, I had to find strong legal arguments against the Institute. I worked day and night with my lawyer, one of the best Designated Senior Counsels in the High Court. We were going through the academic handbook repeatedly. If you read the handbook carefully, you would realise that it was written in quite an incoherent manner with very little proofreading. Points contradicted each other in the same handbook. Anyway, I had found my legal argument.

According to **clause 4.2.4** of the PGP Academic Handbook 2016-18, *A student will be eligible for the Award of the* ***IIM's Diploma*** *on completion of the Programme only if he/she satisfies the following criteria at the end of the second year:*

a) Obtains a ***CGPA*** *of at least 2.0 (i.e., equivalent to C Grade) overall*

I had a CGPA of **3.18** at the end of the second year (including grades from Terms 1, 2, 3, 4, and 6).

According to **clause 4.1.13** of the handbook, "*For PGP students participating in International Students Exchange Programmes of the Institute, the final CGPA is computed on the basis of the courses attended at the IIM only.*"

So, grades from Term 5 were out of the picture. Hence, I was fulfilling this condition by all means.

b) *Does not have more than 8 DCPs in the Second Year (PGP II) of the Programme*

I had **0 DCPs** in both years. DCPs (Deficit Credit Points) are awarded to students who fail a course at the institute.

C) *Does not have any outstanding financial liabilities with the Institute*

I had already submitted my **No Dues Certificate,** duly signed by all Departments.

Hence, in the given scenario, I was fulfilling all the criteria to graduate with my batchmates on 7th April 2018. After allowing me to write my Term VI exams, the Institute had no power to withhold my diploma.

I was prepared to go to court. Let me make you aware of the fact that the courts very rarely interfere in academic matters. But, in poker terminology, I was pot-committed, short-stacked, and even ahead on the turn. I had to go all in to see the river. Folding just didn't make sense. To put it simply, what did I have to lose? The institute might have gone back on their word again (although in writing this time) and would have asked me to repeat Term VI also. I was okay with it. That's the most they could have done. I could live with myself if the court didn't interfere to help me, but not with the regret of not fighting back and accepting injustice with folded hands.

Like the legend, Michael Jordan taught us, "I can accept failure. Everyone fails at something. But I cannot accept not trying." I had already invested so much time and energy into this. It was totally against my education to give up at this point.

All-In

"You can't control other people; you can only control your reaction towards them." Easy to say, unbelievably tough to implement. All the anger, all the frustration, would have been a waste if I had not channelled my energy in the right direction. I had to think through and take calculated steps while moving forward. My lawyer finally filed a writ petition in the High Court on 6th April 2018. Our admission hearing was scheduled for the same day.

A legal battle against a top institute in the country at the young age of 23 was way too overwhelming for me. I just kept my calm and entered the High Court. Realising that I didn't have the physical presence of Papa by my side was too hard to accept. I had to release the anxiety. I found a quiet corner in the lobby of the ground floor of the High Court and broke down while writing to my dad.

"Papa, as I walked past the main gate of the High Court for the first time, I suddenly felt your hand on my shoulder, with you walking by my side. I somehow controlled my tears as I didn't want to appear weak in front of my lawyer. I will be forever grateful to you for making me strong and mature to handle such intense situations but I had never imagined I would have to do this without you. I had always been on the back side, with you making decisions for me. Suddenly I find myself without your guidance and it's the most unsettling realisation to come to terms with. Tomorrow—7th April 2018—is the date you had been looking forward to, even more than I have, the convocation, where you wanted to see me graduate with flying colours. Destiny does play with us like mere puppets. I neither have you nor am I being allowed to graduate on this Convocation Day. But I promise you this Papa, I will never give up. I will keep fighting for what I believe in and what I deserve. Love You."

The admission hearing happened after lunch. In the courtroom, I was sitting on one of the benches in the back with at least 50 other people in the room. Only the lawyers go to the front row and interact with the Judge. The eagerness when my case no. got called out made me involuntarily adjust my hair and collar, even when I was not in the vicinity of the Judge. The case was accepted and the scheduled date for the next hearing was 12th April when the institute was supposed to present a counter.

Here, I would like to thank Leah, my senior from the IIM, my mentor, and my colleague at Silverlight during the Internship. I was constantly in touch with her related to my case and she was as supportive as anybody else could ever be. She remarked, "Sid, every cloud has a silver lining is what people say, but they forget to mention that oftentimes you have to draw that lining yourself."

Maa consoled me, "Siddharth, no matter what the outcome is, you will eventually emerge as a human being who is better equipped to deal with any kind of adversity in the future." I gathered some courage and got myself together. And this was the moment when I decided to start writing this book.

I was getting exposed to the workings of our legal system, first-hand, and I started making sure that I was learning as much as I could. I was meeting with the best of lawyers and learning the intricacies involved in pursuing a lawsuit in our country.

Waiting for the next hearing from the 6th to the 12th of April changed me. It made me realise that when you give your 100% into a situation, the outcome stops making any difference. By going all-in, you make yourself strong enough to walk unscathed out of a situation, no matter the result. You are at least able to bless yourself with HOPE. Even if the outcome is negative for that particular episode, it makes you better prepared to fight your future battles. You are in a better position to understand your mistakes and anticipate the grave consequences that they can initiate. Maybe I had started drawing a faint silver line for myself.

The hearing happened on 12th April and as expected, the institute's counsel asked for more time to file a counter. Since vacation was scheduled for the court from 14th April - 20th May, the matter got postponed to 22nd May. Strangely, I had become more tolerant of the system by now.

Puppets of Destiny

The wait for the next court hearing tested my tolerance exhaustively. In addition to that, even though technically I had a very strong case, there were two important things against me. One, courts usually don't interfere in academic matters. So, it was of utmost importance that the judge was willing to hear the case out and had the spine to take a strong stand for what was right.

Second, I did not have time by my side. My 5th term was supposed to start in September 2018 and for that, choosing electives and other processes were supposed to start in July. If the court verdict hadn't come before that, I would have had to drop the case. I couldn't risk foregoing Term V and continue fighting the case with an uncertain outcome. Risking the degree would have made the entire struggle futile.

I was losing a lot in monetary terms too. I was losing the hefty salary I would have gotten from Silverlight. I would have had to pay the Term V fees again in case I lost the case. There was this outstanding education loan. Along with that, Silverlight sends all the new joiners to New York for around three weeks for the New Bankers' Training Program. It might sound immature, but to me personally, this program was a major attraction from Silverlight. Living in one of the most happening cities in the world, with the wittiest minds and within the core of the investment banking universe, sounded like a dream. I would have missed this or at least got it deferred to the next year.

I had travelled across many countries by now, but the United States remained unticked on my bucket list. Papa had seen times of sheer poverty and got himself out of it. Sending his son to the US once, was the typical middle-class dream he had had, just like other fathers of his generation. This was the fourth time that an opportunity to go to the US had knocked on my door and got turned away.

First, I was in the seventh standard and my school, DPS Bhilai, had a tie-up with an educational travel company. The school was sending a group of students to the US including a visit to the NASA space station. It was costly, but the way my parents had raised me, I thought money was the last thing I should be worried about. I went to my Dad with all the excitement in the world, "Papa, the school is sending us to NASA and many other places in the US for an educational trip."

Papa displayed mixed emotions, but I was too young to understand, "Ok, how much is the cost?"

"Around 2.5 lakhs for 12 days."

Papa sighed, "It's not worth it Beta. We will go to the US some other time and we will all go together."

"But Papa, this is a once-in-a-lifetime opportunity. This is priceless and a school trip will always be different from a family trip."

"No, you are too young, and also, the exorbitant cost does not make sense."

"Papa, I will have a team of teachers accompanying me, so safety is not a concern. Plus, if we have the money, how does it matter if the trip is rightly priced or not?"

For Papa, money was just a number; if he felt something was good, he was always ready to spend on it.

In a sterner voice now, he exclaimed, "No, beta. You are not mature enough to understand and you can't go to the US now."

I was angry and irritated, more because Papa always believed in "Convince or get convinced." He had not convinced me, and he knew that. There was something he was not telling me. Some of my close friends were going and I was too young to not be upset about it.

A couple of days later, I got to know the whole story from Mom. This was somewhere around the 2007-08 recession and I had no idea that my family had suffered a huge loss in the business. Papa never shared his business worries with the kids. More than me, Papa was regretting not being able to send me to the US. The silent emotions fathers hide within themselves just leave me with a feeling of awe and admiration.

The second instance, I was in my 3rd year of Engineering (2015). My college had a tie-up with Rutgers University in New Jersey, USA for a summer program of 2 months. It was pretty costly, but my father had the money now and he was ready and excited to send me there. This was the exact time when students went for summer internships. I had made up my mind to let go of the corporate internship and choose this program instead. But, are we anything more than mere puppets of our destiny? There came an opportunity I could not let go of. Morgan Stanley came to our campus to offer a summer internship at its Bangalore office. Being a stockbroker's son, getting exposure at Morgan Stanley was quite exciting. It was one of the most sought-after roles on campus and the chances of converting that role were bleak. As far as the Rutgers Program was concerned, paying by myself and going to the USA was something I could do later in my life.

The first round was a coding round. Around 350 students took that test and 25 were shortlisted for the interview round. I was one of them. We were supposed to wait in the conference room until we were called for the interview. Now, everybody knows nerds, right? They found a whiteboard in the conference room and started discussing some out-of-the-world tree algorithms I had never heard of. My chances of getting through the interview round were even fainter now. The competition was fierce. I gathered two of my friends and started clicking some pictures in the conference room as a memory. It felt good to reach the top 25 for the interview round and I wanted to feel happy about it, no matter the result of the impending round.

Soon, I was called for my interview. Before entering the room, I just told myself, "The fact that these toppers know more than me is known only to me, not to the interviewer. The interviewer will only know what is effectively conveyed to him, and my communication skills are better than theirs. I have to give my 100%." The interview went decently well, both in terms of technical and general questions. But while others were called for the second round, I wasn't. I was a little confused and disappointed, but never mind, it was worth a try.

I started preparing myself for the Rutgers Program in the USA. One fine morning, I received a call from the Placements' Office. "Hey Siddharth, Congratulations! You have been offered an internship by Morgan Stanley." I was dumbstruck, I could not believe my ears. I was not even called for the second round of interviews. Could one interview be so good that a single interviewer was able to convince the entire team to hire the interviewee? Confidence and persistence do pay off. Only 5 people were selected finally.

And this was the second time my US trip got cancelled.

Third, I had gotten admission offer letters from both SPJIMR (Finance) and a premier IIM for my post-graduation (both colleges were very close to each other in terms of their rankings). As a part of the SPJIMR program, all finance students needed to go to Cornell University, New York for three weeks as a part of their Global Fast Track program. With a heavy heart, I let go of that opportunity too when I chose the IIM over SPJIMR because of the brand and a better campus life among other things.

When it was about to get cancelled for the fourth time, it was inevitably depressing. The first three times when I had let go of that opportunity, it was a calculated choice every time, but this time, it was not under my control. I just couldn't avoid the circumstances. I had worked day and night to get that PPO from Silverlight and I deserved to go on that New Bankers' Training Program by all means. Sometimes, even when you understand that life is unfair, it is hard for you to accept it. I understand that it's not a big deal for somebody to go to the States but it was important for me. It was a part of the dream my dad had seen for me. Even during the last stages of his cancer, I once told him, "Papa, let me just come back to Bhilai the moment I complete my MBA. We will do business together, let's leave the job offer." His instant reply was, "No, you shouldn't forgo the opportunity to attend the New Bankers' Training Program of Silverlight in the USA. You have to get that exposure. After that, you can return to Bhilai and we will do whatever you feel is right."

I was sitting at home, with nothing left to do, as the court took its own time. I was one of the first few people in the batch to get an internship and the subsequent PPO and there I stood, stuck, at a dead end. I was running so fast and suddenly, a rope pulled me back. Still frantically trying to move forward but to no avail.

Blessing in Disguise

The worst psychological state of mind is to have a superiority complex and an inferior status. I was at the top for as long as I could remember, the sudden fall was intractable. Those 0.4 marks kept revolving in my head and it kept making things worse for me. A few days after I returned from Kochi, I broke down again. I just could not control my emotions. Missing Papa and regretting the situation I had landed myself into, I was at the lowest point in my life.

One gloomy evening, I was lying half-stretched across the study table in my room, feeling utterly dejected by my situation. Incidentally, I happened to glance at my Undergrad Convocation picture with Papa, which was resting on the corner of my table. I thought of the time in college after Papa's death when I had promised myself that I would work incessantly towards becoming an individual Papa would have been proud of. I wondered,

"Would he be proud of the person I am becoming now? Would he be proud of seeing me dejected like this?" I could not see that picture for long, which, in a way, gave me my answer. I got up and decided never to feel pity for myself again. The moment I was getting up, Mom entered my room, "Siddharth, you were running very fast, working hard and achieving whatever you aimed for. Suddenly, destiny is holding you back to see how you react in an unfavourable situation. Times are going to change, sooner or later. What's being tested right now is if you can survive these trying times gracefully and prepare yourself to make the best out of better times in the future." I hugged my Mom tight. I felt like I was reborn after this conversation, owing even my second life to my mother. I started finding the positives in my situation. Never in my dreams had I imagined that even in a situation like this, there could be more positives than negatives.

First, I was getting to spend time with my Mom when she needed it the most. She was the one who was most affected by Papa's death and there was no measure of the degree of her loneliness. Mom never explicitly told me or Kanishka (who was pursuing Fashion Designing in Pune) that we should return to Bhilai because she didn't want us to sacrifice our careers for her. But I could sense it, she needed us with her. Even for me, it was of utmost importance that I spent time with my Mom and the entire family. The best part was that Silverlight had not revoked the offer, so I could still join after November. Even if I had gotten my degree on 7th April 2018, I would have happily accepted some delay in joining Silverlight to spend time with my family. The loan instalments were anyway about to start in January 2019.

Second, I had wanted to try teaching as a profession for a very long time. I had always been in awe of how my favourite teachers used to connect with their audiences. I too wanted to test my communication and guidance skills similarly. Just never got the time and opportunity to pursue it. Now, I felt like a free bird. I went to meet the head of a CAT coaching Institute in Bhilai. I told him my entire story and asked him if I could join as a faculty and prepare students for CAT. I wanted to help students from different backgrounds with common apprehensions and doubts related to the most competitive exam in India. I believed I could connect with them well, being from the same generation and having been through the same journey. He was more than happy to hire me, "We usually don't get IIM people to train students here. It's a pleasure to have you with us." He asked me to give a demo class, suggested some tweaks, and bang! I began teaching.

I had never realised that teaching could be such a tiring job. But the more effort I put in, the more satisfied my students were. Just knowing stuff is not enough, you need to match the frequencies of your students and then explain the concepts. That is why teaching is an art. I could see the results in the rising performance of the students and this happiness was something I had not experienced often before. Sure I was getting paid for my job, but this wasn't about money. The happiness came from being able to make a difference and from being able to pass the knowledge I had acquired for the betterment of my students. Soon, we organised some seminars for both parents and students, covering multiple MBA entrance exams. I was savouring every moment.

Third, my family business needed some attention. After Papa's loss, it had been extremely difficult for my uncles to switch back to normalcy. The company's head office was due for renovation and there were a lot of business expansion opportunities that required some contemplation. The situation gave me time to assist my uncles and share insights from my exposure and education. The best thing about working with my uncles and dad is that their decision-making always works on logic. The "Convince or get convinced" philosophy was not just my father's anthem, it's also my uncles'. It was pretty easy to match the frequency of my ideas with theirs. Also, the moral support and the strength that came from standing together immensely helped us deal with our current situation.

Fourth, I had never given enough attention to my health. I was not obese, but overweight. This was the perfect time to take care of my health. Had I taken up the job, with the hectic investment banking schedule, I would have rarely gotten the time to work out. I immediately joined the gym. I was hitting the gym consistently and the results just kept motivating me to continue the hard work. A good 1.5-hour session in the gym helped me release stress and increase my happiness quotient at the same time. The only target in the gym was to beat my performance of the previous day. I wish we could learn to apply this to life too.

Fifth, I got the time to write this book. I had wanted to write a book that motivates the youth of the country in some way, for a very long time. I had even begun writing one during my 2nd year of Engineering but never really got the time to wholeheartedly focus on that book. The free time now allowed me to observe the everyday situations around us from multiple points of view. I could focus on this book and narrate the zillion stories I had always wanted to. The comfort of living at home offered the much-needed freshness of mind while consolidating and creating content for the book.

What was I losing in my situation?

First, I would have had to pay the Term V fees again, in case the college didn't accept my request for a fee waiver. That would have been around 3 lakhs. I guess I could live with it. I could have used it as another motivation to work harder.

Second, I had to attend four more courses and spend three more months in college. I could easily deal with that. Apart from getting to learn something from the four courses, spending time at the Institute would have been a welcome break after pursuing multiple tasks simultaneously during the break. Who would anyway mind spending time in God's Own Campus? The campus was a heavenly resort. We had a gym too, perfect to continue working on my fitness goals.

It was just the positives from then on. I guess it's just the simple difference between viewing the glass as half empty or half full, after all. Apart from the tangible facts that could be readily counted, I became stronger in terms of dealing with the loss of Papa's physical presence from our lives. There is a famous dialogue from the Bollywood Blockbuster *Anand*, where Rajesh Khanna tells Amitabh Bachchan, "Babumoshai, Zindagi badi honi chahiye, lambi nahi". My father was a perfect example of this. He was not born with a silver spoon, but he made sure that I was born with one. From living in a small rented house to building a bungalow the size of a palace with a personal elevator and a Mercedes on the porch, he had proved that hard work and ethics take you a long way. I could never stop missing his presence, but now I shifted to celebrating his inspiring life rather than crying about his departure. His teachings were ingrained in me. I embraced them and felt it was my duty to pass them on to future generations.

He believed that the most important step to achieving big in life is to stop playing small. You cannot allow yourself to put a cap on your dreams. I had planned to achieve so many things with my dad. Now, I had to push myself to fulfil them, both for myself and for him. My mother's happiness now was in seeing me and Kanishka grow as individuals in our lives. I was backed against the wall, but I had to fight back. I had to either break the wall behind me and explore a new path or keep fighting back until the force pushing me to the wall gave up. My giving up was out of the picture. The best part, my family was proud of the way I was dealing with my situation. They made sure that I was always surrounded by positivity and motivation. And yes, after being on antidepressants for almost a month, I didn't need them anymore, no more anxiety attacks.

Rising from a Fall

The first step in fighting the force that is pushing you against the wall is regaining your lost confidence. And your confidence sure takes a hit when Murphy's Law starts defining your life. Who was I to be spared? With a series of unfavourable circumstances for months together, I had become accustomed to expecting the worst.

By this time, I had stopped playing poker, both offline and online. My risk-taking capacity had reached a new low. It had started affecting my game adversely. A lot of you might think that since poker involves taking risks, it is similar to gambling, but these risks are not mere coin flips. These are purely calculated risks. I had changed from a tight aggressive player to a tight passive player. I was only playing when I had nuts (the best hand) and it had become very easy for my opponents to bluff me out. The ability to play aggressively and take a stab at the pots with calculated risks was gone.

I had to stop playing poker until I could get my mind straight. When you are facing a downswing (series of losses) in poker, you have to take a break. You should only return when you can play without any biases. When you are playing poker, you have to only play poker. This is true for both positive and negative mindsets. You can't let your game get affected by happiness or sadness related to other parts of your life.

Even in everyday activities like driving, more than the pleasure of driving a Mercedes, I was anxious about driving it safely. There was no joy, just the fear of banging the car somewhere. I used to be a guy who would enjoy the smallest of moments, but now, I was just afraid of things going wrong at every step.

Teaching CAT aspirants, gymming, and writing this book helped but I was yet to fully regain my lost confidence. I first had to think clearly about what I wanted to achieve and how to work towards achieving it. I made a list of life goals and started contemplating them. I realised that I was committing one of the biggest blunders of my life. I was planning to pursue a career I had never wanted for myself. I was just going with the wind, overwhelmed by the job offer from one of the best investment banking firms in the world.

Remember how I fought with my dad before doing an MBA? I had wanted to be an entrepreneur but eventually got convinced that the wiser thing would be to get a stamp of credibility from an IIM first and then pursue my entrepreneurial dreams. This was my time. The wait for the degree was almost over and I was free to explore new business ventures. Being so entangled in the institutional web, I had almost lost sight of my long-term goals.

A job at Silverlight would have given me exposure. But then, there is no limit to exposure. By staying in Bangalore for 4 years, spending 2 years at an IIM, starting my company, internships with Morgan Stanley, Silverlight, Bidstalk (a start-up), and SAIL (a government organisation), travelling across Europe for three months, dealing with bureaucracy and suing an IIM, I had already gained a decent amount of exposure. Moreover, entrepreneurs always find ways to get exposure, no matter the environment.

Had I not been clear about entrepreneurship, it would have made sense to join Silverlight for some time and then decide. But when it was crystal clear to me that this was what I had always wanted to do, there was no point waiting for another 2 years. These 2 years could be used to build a strong base in the industries of my new business ventures, build contacts, and reconnect with people I had known in the past.

Even though I kept thinking of the situation logically, at one point I simply thought, "Does anything else even matter if I can't be with Maa when she needs me the most?" She had completely lost her support system after Papa. Having my own business could at least give me the freedom to choose where to stay and settle down.

On 13th May 2018, Mother's Day, I told my mother, "Maa, I am planning to let go of Silverlight. I will stay here with you and work on my entrepreneurial dreams." She revolted, "Siddharth, I know you are doing this for me. Don't spoil your career because of me." I surely knew that she wanted me to be with her, yet, she put my career above her wants. Can we ever come close to matching what mothers do for us?

Ironically, the more educated one is, the lesser one's risk-taking capacity tends to become. I decided to believe in my education and capabilities and chose to stay put with my decision. The best thing that came out of this tussle was the fact that I got in touch with my inner self. I was an entrepreneur at heart. For the first time in a very long time, I was truly convinced and happy about my decision. The resulting determination to work was inevitable. Suddenly, I felt like I had grown wings. Entrepreneurship gave me those wings. I decided to use my time till the completion of the 5th trimester in November to do research on which entrepreneurial venture I should eventually start working on. Whether it would be revisiting one of my past ideas or starting something from scratch.

The foundation behind choosing to pursue entrepreneurship was strong and hence the resulting motivation to give it my blood and sweat. After all, wasn't this the dream I had always seen? The dream to work tirelessly for my entrepreneurial ambitions? The experience in the last few months had only made me stronger and I had started paving my path towards living the dream.

Losing Small vs Winning Big

In the blink of an eye, it was time for Term V registration. The institute kept asking for continuances and took more than two months to file a counter in court. The court took its own time and there was no verdict yet. I emailed the Institute to allow me to register for Term V. I received a reply from the PGP office saying that since the matter was sub judice (in court), no action could be taken on my request. Essentially meaning, "Withdraw the case if you want to register for Term V." I discussed it with my lawyer. He said, "Even though you have a strong case, the Judge needs to be inclined to understand the technicalities involved in the case and rule in your favour. It is easy for me to recommend that you should keep fighting the case and earn even more in fees from you. But practically speaking, given the delay with which the institute is responding, this is going to take a lot more time than expected. With your Term V registration at stake now, I would suggest that you withdraw the case and complete your Term there. You can't risk losing both the degree and the case."

This is when the character Frank Galvin's dialogue from the movie "The Verdict" started making sense to me, "Courts are not there to give you justice. They are there to give you a chance at justice."

I decided to follow my lawyer's advice and withdrew the case. I wish I had won the case, but I realised that I had to understand the difference between giving up and moving on. I was not giving up, I was making a good fold and moving on. But the minute I withdrew my case, there was a bunch of "intellectuals" (including some friends) who were just waiting to say, "I had told you so, court cases never help, you should have just accepted the Institute's decision." In those moments, I realised that there are two kinds of people, first, those who want to lose small and second, those who want to win big. I belonged to the second category.

I choose winning big over losing small every single time because other than a dozen ways in which it helps me grow as a person, it keeps my hope intact. It gives me something to look forward to. Let's take the court case for instance. The court's way of operation did make me feel helpless. But that in turn pushed me to pursue things I could have under my control. It proved to be a big motivation for writing this book and for pulling all-nighters for my entrepreneurial dreams. Sometimes, your journey while choosing to win big itself is rewarding enough to compensate for the efforts you put into winning. Choosing to lose small is the easier thing to do. I am confident that even if I fail 99 times out of 100 while trying to win big, that one single win will be a life changer.

I strongly feel that although you cannot control the cards that are dealt to you, you can choose how you play them. People who prefer losing small over winning big end up folding most of the cards dealt to them because that is not what they wanted in the first place. People who prefer winning big, play the hand they are dealt like that is the hand they have always wanted. They never fold until they have put in a genuine effort to make the best out of those cards. My theory was further validated when I read the book "Think and Grow Rich", an all-time International bestseller by Napoleon Hill for self-development and self-improvement. It showcases how a lot of people who have made it big in life turned misfortune into a home run for themselves. They knew that opportunity had a sly habit of slipping by the back door. They were dealt a bad hand but they did not fold. They smartly played the hand with courage, faith, and wits to reach where they are today.

The grass is not greener on the other side; it is greener where you water it. So as long as you are true to yourself while working passionately towards your dreams, sooner or later, you will win, and you will win BIG.

Pivot

It was time to return to the IIM campus, for my Term V. Strangely, I was excited to go back. I have emphasised the beauty and positivity of the campus multiple times. I was in no way ready to miss out on the fun of living in a resort for another three months. But this time, I made sure that I did not stop working on my entrepreneurial goals once I went to campus. I had become successful in rekindling my lost confidence. I was more confident and determined than ever. The administration had changed by then. Thankfully, the new administration paid heed to my multiple appeals for fee reimbursement and my tuition fee was reimbursed.

I resumed playing poker. Almost every alternate weekend during the three months, I used to take an overnight bus to Bangalore to play professional poker in the poker clubs. During my poker escapades, I got introduced to some communities where individuals could stake other poker players and take a proportional return on the player's winnings/losses after subtracting a player's mark-up fees. It was being done through social media posts in online poker groups, in an unorganised manner. I got super excited and the tech geek in me found an opening to enter into the Poker market. I decided to build an automated platform for poker staking. Finally, I found the passion project for my entrepreneurial dream. I concretely conceptualized the idea. Immediately after that, I sent an apology email to Silverlight for not being able to take up their PPO along with an expression of gratitude for standing by me.

To keep my costs low, I started forming a team of coders remotely in Bhilai and took product and project management on my plate. By the time my Term V ended, my PRD (Product Requirement Doc) was ready.

While I was on campus, Silverlight came for its presentation to recruit juniors for the summer internship. I grabbed the opportunity to thank them on stage and tell the juniors about how supportive Silverlight is as an employer. After I was done sharing my internship experiences, Akhilesh (my mentor who had come from Silverlight for the presentation) remarked, "Sid, from the time of your presentations at Silverlight during the internship to the speech you gave today, you have grown exponentially as an individual. I am proud of how you have handled the unfortunate incidents in your recent past and used them to come out stronger. When you were speaking, I was so happy that you were my buddy at Silverlight." The increased confidence had started reflecting off of me.

While I was dealing with all the mess of the foreign exchange grade issue, Silverlight's confidence in me was one of the major uplifters that kept me going. They never revoked my job offer. In fact, during the entire episode, HR kept calling me and taking updates about the proceedings of the court case. It was like they were standing by my side throughout my struggle. I could not join them finally because I chose to be an entrepreneur, but I will always be grateful to them.

Writing this book helped me accept another reality, "Time doesn't heal anything, you just get used to the circumstances." I will wholeheartedly celebrate Papa's life and learn from his deeds but I can never stop missing him. How can you stop missing someone who made you what you are in the first place? Had it not been for Papa's faith in me, I would never have been able to write this book. Even before I started my course at the IIM, he was the one who encouraged me to write a book about my IIM experiences.

After returning to Bhilai after my MBA, I didn't waste any time. I converted the empty hall on my terrace into an office and started building the poker staking platform with my team of 4 coders. Can you miss something you have never had? My entire purpose of becoming more capable as a businessman was to be able to work with Papa one day. I had never worked with him before, but I was still missing working with him every step of the way. To ace businesses like Papa did, I needed to channel these emotions into my work. When I was discussing the implementation of some tricky architectures for the platform with my team, the only question on my mind would be, "What would Papa have done? How would he have found a way around it?" Deep down, I knew that he was with me; watching me as I was rising from the fall. How I wished that all of it was just a bad dream and hoped that when I woke up, Papa was still there.

After 5-6 months of sleepless nights, many 24-hour hackathons, and head-on problem solving, in June'19, MVP (Minimum Viable Product) of "InTheMoney.in"—India's first poker staking platform, was launched. Even across the world, there were only two such platforms, both in the US. While the proof of concept for InTheMoney was yet to be validated, another proof of concept had already been validated in the process—I could get good quality software development done at much lower costs in Bhilai as compared to the metro cities. So as we were testing the waters with InTheMoney, I simultaneously pivoted to doing software development for other companies and added more coders to my team. I started aggressively tapping into my network to land software development projects. It helped a lot with the cash flow. This is how Riverhouse Technologies was born. Today (in 2025), we deal with all kinds of web and mobile applications, custom ERPs, end-to-end tech outsourcing for startups, and resource augmentation. We even have a few products in the market in the automobile and real-estate sector.

Managing Riverhouse does perfect justice to my skill set of computer science Engineering and MBA. Also, it opened my eyes to the bane of students from tier 2 and tier 3 cities who are forced to leave their families for a good career. Like me, there are so many people in my hometown of Bhilai who want to stay close to their families; college grads who don't want to face the hassles of living in a metro city and want to settle down in Bhilai, for good. But most of them have to move out because of a lack of opportunities. I want the change to happen where coders have an option of pursuing their ambitions in Bhilai and I am trying to do my part to help bring about that change.

There are many well-established colleges in Bhilai and even the most talented students from these colleges end up at MNCs in metro cities, many of which indirectly end up inhibiting the freshers' deserved growth by either keeping them on a bench or making them work on in-house/legacy technologies whose experience soon becomes obsolete for the dynamically changing technical world. We make sure that all our developers get exposure to the latest coding frameworks and code in the same languages that are used/designed by the likes of Google and Facebook. It's a boon for professionals who want to excel in the software domain and still stay with their families.

What some professionals lack is good communication and soft skills due to limited exposure and lesser polishing of personality. I have hired experienced mentors to train my team in Bhilai on the same. Using my exposure to the working of top MNCs, I have created a culture in the company that promotes respect for every individual and that makes every employee pay attention to improving her soft skills. The network and the IIM tag have been really helpful in giving me opportunities to bid for innovative projects from time to time and the company has been profitable since the first month of its incorporation.

At Riverhouse, our vision is to provide lucrative opportunities to budding software developers in Bhilai (and nearby areas) and improve the quality of software development as a whole. We respect the individual ambitions of every human resource and our company's growth is measured by the collective growth of our employees. We aim to be a preferred IT workplace in Central India and the first choice of our clients across the globe.

The people happiest with this venture are the parents of employees who have their sons and daughters close to them while still making good money and a career for themselves. Nothing beats the satisfaction of being there for your loved ones through thick and thin. Because of this, out of all the ventures I am pursuing or have pursued in the past, Riverhouse Technologies is the closest to my heart. The success and growth of this company deliver happiness to me in its purest form. InTheMoney eventually died, one because of poor response from the market (the concept was ahead of its time and the poker ecosystem was yet to get more mature to attract volumes) and second because the pivot (Riverhouse) took off well and kept demanding more of my bandwidth.

Life beyond the MBA

Today, I have an MBA degree, branded by the Indian Institute of Management, for life. It did involve a lot of ups and downs and rising from a steep fall but I have zero regrets. The foreign exchange program opened my mind to the outside world in a way I never knew before. The two and a half years of my MBA have only made me stronger and more competent for the rest of my life. I feel blessed to have had these experiences at such a young age. At the end of the day, it was one hell of a ride. So, apart from losing the physical presence of Papa, if given a chance, yes, I would do it all over again.

I wholeheartedly loved my time at my IIM and just because of the ruthless behaviour of a few people, I could not have carried a negative image of the Institute along with me. I will always be proud of being an IIM alumnus. The IIM just didn't teach me Business Administration, it taught me life, and it taught me how to make the best of the cards dealt to me. My time at the IIM proved my father right. When I was facing the dilemma of joining an MBA or entrepreneurship, Papa convinced me to join an MBA and today, I feel more confident than ever about following the path of entrepreneurship. I have started realising the credibility that comes with the brand image of a top IIM. I have a much stronger network of people who are helping me considerably in taking Riverhouse Technologies to the next level. How I wish I could tell Papa today, "You were right Papa, you were right all along. Thanks for pushing me in the right direction."

What is my next heaven? Well, my journey so far has taught me enough to know that life is what you make out of it. I plan to focus on expanding Riverhouse Technologies' physical presence to other tier 2 and tier 3 cities shortly. My dream of going to the United States is still unfulfilled. I dream of finding a business opportunity in the US and staying there for at least a year. I want to devote myself to public services at some point, not because I share a birthday with Donald Trump but because I wish to serve my country proactively. I also want to devote more time to writing and publishing books that can inspire people through my experiences. The dreams do appear to be far-fetched but I just remember what Papa taught me, "If you dream, you may or may not get there. But if you don't, you will never get there."

I have one parting piece of advice to share with all the readers that has helped me grow during every phase of my life,

Don't sell yourself short, ever.

The Roots and the Strength

One of the most underappreciated things in life is good parenting. More often than not, we take the efforts and sacrifices our parents make for our upbringing for granted. Although we can never thank our parents enough, this letter was a small effort towards extending heartfelt gratitude towards my parents by me and my sister. We had narrated it to them on their anniversary a year before Papa passed away. I feel that sharing this letter with my readers is the perfect way to give closure to this book and say cheers to a new beginning!

Dearest Maa and Papa,

Out of all the things in life that matter, the most important to us is our bond with you, nothing has ever been more valuable to us. And we say this at the risk of sounding clichéd, the bond is irreplaceable. There is no bond as divine and selfless as the one we share with you. Though we rarely acknowledge it explicitly, we always understand and are grateful for all the sacrifices you make for us. In addition to the materialistic luxuries in life, which a lot of parents can deliver, you make an extraordinary effort to teach life to us.

Consciously or subconsciously, your parenting taught us how to value the most important aspects of life, the value of hard-earned money, and the pleasure of selflessly loving your near and dear ones. You taught us how to respect other people and to make ourselves respectable. Instead of imposing your opinions on us out of authority, you allowed us to make our own decisions and question the authenticity of ubiquitous distractions and opportunities. You taught us never to undermine our capabilities and to never think of ourselves as inferior to anybody else. Eventually, all of it inculcated a beautiful thinking power within us, the power that made us mature and capable of being independent and successful in life. The power enables us to lead people and never be afraid of walking alone.

Papa, we inherited the prudent and bold traits from you, and Maa, you taught us humility, you taught us how to win people over, people of any age, of any status. The combination that the two of you together possess, in addition to complimenting each other, perfectly helped us in moulding ourselves. Now, we have a fair sense of judgement on the everyday issues in life, however big or small they may be. The ethics and values that have been sown into our subconscious help us to radiate a strong character and further strengthen our credibility in the minds of other people. Our upbringing makes sure that we do not hurt innocent souls even unintentionally and also are not naïve to let ourselves be hurt by people who try to pull us down. It teaches us not to get swayed by general opinion and to stick to the efforts needed to meet our goals.

Today, we stand tall, ready to face the real world and carry forward the legacy defined by both of you. And the strength to do that comes from the utmost faith in our ROOTS. Today, we shine with immense confidence and courage to face and conquer any challenge. Our roots have always motivated us to take that extra leap of faith while facing the harshest of obstacles that stop us from inching closer to our goals. Our roots have taught us to take a stand for what is right and never be afraid of taking the road less travelled. This has time and again encouraged us to separate ourselves from the herd and follow our hearts.

We are and will always be grateful for being your children and privileged to be inheriting a heritage that stems from the two of you.

- Loads of Love (Kanishka and Siddharth)

Acknowledgements

My parents, Geetika and Praduman Jain, for raising me the way they did and for unconditionally loving me.

My wife, Arpita Jain, who shines as the brightest light in my life and gives me the courage to pursue my dreams unapologetically.

My son, Ansh Jain, who makes me believe in the power of good karma.

My cousins, Aarushi Jain, and Vedant Jain, and my friends, Mohit Parikh (Author of Manan), and Saurabh Patle, for helping me with proofreading, editing, sanity, and flow check of the book. I believe their constructive feedback improved my story's presentation and made it more engaging for the readers.

My sister, Kanishka Jain, who has always been my biggest cheerleader, and believes in me even when I don't.